Conference on Empirical Methods in Natural Language Processing (EMNLP 2020)

Tutorial Abstracts

Online
19 – 20 November 2020

ISBN: 978-1-7138-1981-3

Printed from e-media with permission by:

Curran Associates, Inc.
57 Morehouse Lane
Red Hook, NY 12571

CURRAN ASSOCIATES INC. proceedings.com

Some format issues inherent in the e-media version may also appear in this print version.

Printed with permission by Curran Associates, Inc. (2021)

Association for Computational Linguistics
209 N. Eighth Street
Stroudsburg, Pennsylvania 18360

Phone: 1-570-476-8006
Fax: 1-570-476-0860

acl@aclweb.org

Additional copies of this publication are available from:

Curran Associates, Inc.
57 Morehouse Lane
Red Hook, NY 12571 USA
Phone: 845-758-0400
Fax: 845-758-2633
Email: curran@proceedings.com
Web: www.proceedings.com

EMNLP 2020

The 2020 Conference on Empirical Methods in Natural Language Processing

Tutorial Abstracts

November 19 - 20, 2020

Introduction

Welcome to the Tutorials Session of EMNLP 2020.

The EMNLP tutorials session in 2020 includes courses on a variety of topics reflecting recent advances in Natural Language Processing methods and applications, especially selected to give conference attendees comprehensive overviews ranging from introductory to cutting-edge topics targeted to wide audience and presented by experts from academia and industry.

This year, continuing the tradition of the past few years, the call, submission, reviewing and selection of tutorials were coordinated jointly for multiple conferences: ACL, AACL-IJCNLP, COLING and EMNLP. The reviewing committee consisted of 19 members, among them the tutorial chairs of the various conferences (Agata Savary and Yue Zhang for ACL, Aline Villavicencio and Benjamin Van Durme for EMNLP, Daniel Beck and Lucia Specia for COLING and Timothy Baldwin and Fei Xia for AACL-IJCNMP), and 11 external reviewers (Emily Bender, Erik Cambria, Gaël Dias, Stefan Evert, Yang Liu, João Sedoc, Xu Sun, Yulia Tsvetkov, Taro Watanabe, Aaron Steven White and Meishan Zhang). Each proposal received 3 reviews, that evaluated criteria including clarity, preparedness, novelty, timeliness, instructors' experience, likely audience, open access to the teaching materials, diversity (multilingualism, gender, age and geolocation) and the compatibility of preferred venues. From the 43 tutorial submissions received, 7 were selected for presentation at EMNLP.

We solicited two types of tutorials, including cutting-edge and introductory themes. From the 7 tutorials accepted for EMNLP, 1 is introductory and 6 are cutting-edge tutorials, all reflecting current topics of interest to the community. The introductory tutorial offers an overview of research in fact-checking, "fake news", and media bias detection (T2). The cutting-edge tutorials present research on methods for interpreting predictions of NLP models (T1), for improving efficiency for high-performance NLP (T3), along with methods for machine reasoning (T4) and spatial language understanding (T5), and the latest advances on applications including simultaneous translation systems (T6) and neural network architectures for text generation (T7).

We would like to thank the ACL, AACL-IJCNLP and COLING tutorial chairs, along with the members of the reviewing committee, who all collaborated to ensure a smooth selection process. Our thanks to the conference organizers for a wonderful and effective collaboration, and in particular to the general chair Bonnie Webber, the website chair Andy MacKinlay, the publicity chairs Anna Rogers and Ruifeng Xu, the ACL anthology director Matt Post, the general publication chair Fei Liu and publication chairs Philippe Muller, Yang Gao and Veronika Laippala, and to the virtual infrastructure chairs Jan-Christoph Klie, Yang Feng, Zhongyu Wei, Eduardo Blanco and Yangsong Feng. Finally, our huge thanks to the tutorial authors for their amazing tutorial proposals, and for their flexibility and collaboration in a period of adaption to virtual conferences.

We hope you enjoy the tutorials.

EMNLP 2020 Tutorial Co-chairs
Aline Villavicencio
Benjamin Van Durme

General Chair

Bonnie Webber, University of Edinburgh, UK

Program Chairs

Trevor Cohn, The University of Melbourne, Australia
Yulan He, University of Warwick, UK
Yang Liu, Amazon – Alexa AI, USA

Tutorial Chairs

Aline Villavicencio, University of Sheffield, UK and Federal University of Rio Grande do Sul, Brazil
Benjamin Van Durme, Johns Hopkins University, USA and Microsoft – Semantic Machines, USA

Table of Contents

Tutorial Program

November 19, 2020

09:00–10:00 *Machine Reasoning: Technology, Dilemma and Future*
Nan Duan, Duyu Tang and Ming Zhou

10:00–11:00 *Fact-Checking, Fake News, Propaganda, and Media Bias: Truth Seeking in the Post-Truth Era*
Preslav Nakov and Giovanni Da San Martino

14:00–15:00 *Fact-Checking, Fake News, Propaganda, and Media Bias: Truth Seeking in the Post-Truth Era*
Preslav Nakov and Giovanni Da San Martino

15:00–19:30 *Interpreting Predictions of NLP Models*
Eric Wallace, Matt Gardner and Sameer Singh

17:00–18:00 *High Performance Natural Language Processing*
Gabriel Ilharco, Cesar Ilharco, Iulia Turc, Tim Dettmers, Felipe Ferreira and Kenton Lee

November 20, 2020

00:00–01:00 *High Performance Natural Language Processing*
Gabriel Ilharco, Cesar Ilharco, Iulia Turc, Tim Dettmers, Felipe Ferreira and Kenton Lee

01:00–02:00 *Machine Reasoning: Technology, Dilemma and Future*
Nan Duan, Duyu Tang and Ming Zhou

17:00–18:00 *Representation, Learning and Reasoning on Spatial Language for Downstream NLP Tasks*
Parisa Kordjamshidi, James Pustejovsky and Marie-Francine Moens

18:00–19:00 *Simultaneous Translation*
Liang Huang, Colin Cherry, Mingbo Ma, Naveen Arivazhagan and Zhongjun He

19:00–20:00 *The Amazing World of Neural Language Generation*
Yangfeng Ji, Antoine Bosselut, Thomas Wolf and Asli Celikyilmaz

November 21, 2020

00:00–01:00 *Representation, Learning and Reasoning on Spatial Language for Downstream NLP Tasks*
Parisa Kordjamshidi, James Pustejovsky and Marie-Francine Moens

01:00–02:00 *Simultaneous Translation*
Liang Huang, Colin Cherry, Mingbo Ma, Naveen Arivazhagan and Zhongjun He

01:00–02:00 *The Amazing World of Neural Language Generation*
Yangfeng Ji, Antoine Bosselut, Thomas Wolf and Asli Celikyilmaz

Cutting-edge Tutorial:
Machine Reasoning: Technology, Dilemma and Future

Nan Duan, Duyu Tang, Ming Zhou
Microsoft Research
{nanduan,dutang,mingzhou}@microsoft.com

1 Introduction

Machine reasoning research aims to build interpretable AI systems that can solve problems or draw conclusions from what they are told (i.e. facts and observations) and already know (i.e. models, common sense and knowledge) under certain constraints. Although its "formal" definitions vary in different publications (McCarthy, 1958; Pearl, 1988; Khardon and Roth, 1994; Bottou, 2011; Bengio, 2019), machine reasoning methods usually share some commonalities. First, such systems are based on different types of **knowledge**, such as logical rules, knowledge graphs, common sense, text evidence, etc. Second, such systems use different **inference algorithms** to manipulate available knowledge for problem-solving. Third, such systems have good **interpretability** to the predictions.

The developments of machine reasoning systems go through several stages. **Symbolic reasoning** methods represent knowledge using symbolic logic (e.g., propositional logic and first order logic) and perform inference using algorithms such as truth-table approach, inference rules approach, resolution, forward chaining and backward chaining. A major defect is that such methods cannot handle the uncertainty in data. **Probabilistic reasoning** methods combine probability and symbolic logic into a unified model. Such methods can deal with uncertainty, but suffer the combinatorial explosion when searching in a large discrete symbolic space. With the rapid developments of deep learning, neural reasoning methods attract much attention. **Neural-symbolic reasoning** methods represent knowledge symbols (such as entities, relationships, actions, logical functions and formulas) as vector or tensor representations, and allow the model to perform end-to-end learning effectively as all components are differentiable. **Neural-evidence reasoning** methods allow the model to communicate with the environment to acquire evidence for reasoning. As such models assume the reasoning layer is not required to be logical, both structured and unstructured data can be used as knowledge. Besides, as the interaction with the environment can be conducted multiple times, such approaches are good at solving sequential decision-making problems.

However, existing machine reasoning methods face with a **dilemma**: although they have many merits such as good abstraction, generalization and interpretability, their performance are still worse than black-box neural networks (such as pre-trained models) on most downstream tasks such as question answering, text classification, etc.

In this tutorial, we will review typical machine reasoning frameworks and talk about the dilemma between black-box neural networks with state-of-the-art performance and machine reasoning methods with better interpretability. We will also discuss possible research directions to escape this dilemma as the future work.

2 Description

We first review four machine reasoning frameworks.

Symbolic Reasoning This approach, also known as the Good, Old-Fashioned AI (GOFAI), was the dominant paradigm in the AI community before the late 1980s. By manipulating knowledge in the form of symbolic logic using inference algorithms, a symbolic reasoning system can solve deductive and inductive reasoning tasks. We will use deductive reasoning as an example to show how this task can be solved based on knowledge in the form of propositional logic and first-order logic, respectively. This part is also closely related to probabilistic reasoning and neural-symbolic reasoning.

Probabilistic Reasoning One drawback of symbolic reasoning is that it cannot handle data un-

Proceedings of the 2020 Conference on Empirical Methods in Natural Language Processing: Tutorial Abstracts, pages 1–6
Online, November 19 - 20, 2020.
https://doi.org/10.18653/v1/P17

certainty. To alleviate this problem, probabilistic reasoning is proposed, which integrates probabilistic models with symbolic knowledge in a unified framework. In such systems, probabilistic models handle the uncertainty issue while the symbolic logic represents types, relations, and the complex dependencies between them. We will use Bayesian Network (Pearl, 1988) and Markov Logic Network (Richardson and Domingos, 2006) as two representative models to show how probabilistic reasoning can solve typical reasoning tasks, such as diagnosis, prediction and maximum probable explanation.

Neural-Symbolic Reasoning Both symbolic reasoning and probabilistic reasoning support strong abstraction and generalization. Such systems have good interpretability but are fragile and inflexible duo to the finite and discrete symbolic representations. On the contrary, neural network models achieve state-of-the-art performance on various AI tasks, due to their good representation and learning capabilities. However, such models cannot capture compositionality and generalization in a systematic way. They cannot provide explicit decision-making evidence to explain their outputs as well, which make such systems look like a black box. So it is straightforward to integrate neural networks with symbolic reasoning, which is called neural-symbolic reasoning in this tutorial. In general, a neural-symbolic reasoning system (1) integrates existing reasoning technologies with symbolic knowledge based on neural networks and (2) implements inference as a chain of differentiable modules, where each module represents a program with a specific function. By doing these, such systems are usually more interpretable than black-box neural networks. We will review knowledge graph reasoning (Bordes et al., 2013; Wang et al., 2014; Lin et al., 2015; Wang et al., 2017; Glorot et al., 2013; Socher et al., 2013; Dong et al., 2014; Liu et al., 2016; Dettmers et al., 2018; Guo et al., 2019; Ren et al., 2020; Xiong et al., 2017; Dong et al., 2019; Rocktäschel and Riedel, 2017; Qu and Tang, 2019; K. Teru et al., 2020), neural semantic parsing (Dong and Lapata, 2016, 2018; Sun et al., 2018; Guo et al., 2018; Mao et al., 2019; Zhong et al., 2020), neural module network (Andreas et al., 2016; Hu et al., 2017; Gupta et al., 2020; Chen et al., 2020) and symbolic knowledge as constraints (Rocktaschel et al., 2015; Hu et al., 2016; Xu et al., 2018; Li and Srikumar, 2019; Wang et al., 2020) as four representative models.

Neural-Evidence Reasoning Previously mentioned three reasoning pipelines have the merits of utilizing abstractive logical or symbolic functions, which are interpretable to developers and users at concept level. The design of such symbolic functions in real applications are typically conducted by domain experts, thus these models cannot be easily extend to broader applications. Here, we review neural-evidence models that find external evidence and combine evidence with the input to make predictions. We group existing methods into three categories, including unstructured textual evidence retrieval models, structured fact evidence retrieval models, and iterative evidence retrieval models. Applications include open question answering (Chen and Yih, 2020), CommonsenseQA (Talmor et al., 2019), fact checking and verification (Thorne et al., 2018), inferential text generation (Rashkin et al., 2018; Sap et al., 2019), and multi-hop question answering (Yang et al., 2018).

We then talk about the dilemma between black-box neural networks with state-of-the-art performance and machine reasoning approaches with better interpretability.

Dilemma: Interpretability vs. Performance Despite the appealing properties of the previously mentioned machine reasoning approaches in terms of interpretability, the reality is that the leading systems on open benchmarks, evaluated by accuracy, are typically black-box models. We will discuss this dilemma of "interpretability versus performance" by showing the empirical success of pre-trained models on natural language understanding challenges, including Grade 8 New York Regents science exam (Clark et al., 2019), discrete reasoning over natural language (Dua et al., 2019), reasoning over rules in natural language (Clark et al., 2020), and logical reasoning (Yu et al., 2020). Afterwards, we will review model interpretation methods, including post-hoc ones and intrinsic ones. Post-hoc methods aim to interpret what an existing model learned without making changes to the original model. We will cover saliency maps (Simonyan et al., 2013), local interpretable model-agnostic explanations (LIME) (Ribeiro et al., 2016), testing with concept activation vectors (TCAV) (Kim et al., 2018), and visual explanation generation (Hendricks et al., 2016). Intrinsic methods are that inherently interpretable (to some extent). We will cover attention (Bahdanau et al., 2014), interpretable CNN (Zhang et al., 2018), and neural module network (Andreas et al., 2016).

We last summarize the content of this tutorial and discuss possible future directions.

Summary This tutorial classifies machine reasoning methods into 4 categories based on their modeling mechanisms, including symbolic reasoning, probabilistic reasoning, neural-symbolic reasoning and neural-evidence reasoning. Symbolic reasoning can handle complex reasoning tasks by using logical rules. Probabilistic reasoning further alleviates the data uncertainty issue in symbolic reasoning systems by introducing probabilistic models. Neural-symbolic reasoning provides more robust representation and learning capabilities based on the latest deep learning technologies. Neural-evidence reasoning doesn't require the reasoning layer to be logical, so they can leverage both symbolic and non-symbolic evidence. All these methods have good applications in many real-world scenarios like expert system, medical diagnosis, knowledge base completion, question answering, search engine, fact checking, etc.

Of course, we also notice the dilemma of existing machine reasoning methods. We think this is only a short-term phenomenon. With the continue and rapid developments of different areas at the same time, such as knowledge base engineering, pre-training, interpretability modeling and neural-symbolic computing, we believe machine reasoning will definitely have a brighter future.

3 Outline

Opening (15 min.) will describe the motivation and outline of this tutorial and give our definition on machine reasoning.

Symbolic Reasoning (20 min.) will review typical methods based on propositional logic and first order logic, respectively.

Probabilistic Reasoning (20 min.) will review typical methods based on Bayesian Network and Markov Logic Network, respectively.

Neural-Symbolic Reasoning (40 min.) will review typical methods including knowledge graph reasoning, neural semantic parsing, neural module network and symbolic knowledge as constraints.

Neural-Evidence Reasoning (40 min.) will review text-base evidence retrieval models, fact-based evidence retrieval models, and interactive evidence retrieval models.

Dilemma: Interpretability vs. Performance (30 min.) will review post-hoc models and intrinsic models for interpretation, and discuss the dilemma of "interpretability versus performance".

Summary & Future Discussion (10 min.) will summarize the content of this tutorial and discuss possible future directions.

4 Prerequisites for the Attendees

We expect the attendees to be familiar with typical NLP tasks (such as question answering, semantic parsing, text generation, etc.), basic concepts of logic (such as propositional logic and first order logic) and knowledge graph, recent neural network architectures (such as convolutional neural network, recurrent neural network and Transformer) and pre-trained language models (such as GPT and BERT).

5 Small Reading List

- Domingos and Richardson (2004) - an introduction to Markov Logic as a unifying framework for statistical relational learning, which is closely related to probabilistic reasoning;
- Bottou (2011) - a nice introduction to machine reasoning;
- Besold et al. (2017) and Garcez et al. (2019) - two surveys on neural-symbolic reasoning;
- Storks et al. (2019) - a survey on benchmarks, knowledge resources, learning and inference approaches to natural language inference;
- Du et al. (2020) - a survey on interpretable machine learning techniques;
- Chen and Yih (2020) - a tutorial on open-domain question answering, in which many work can be categorized as neural-evidence reasoning;
- Sap et al. (2020) - a tutorial on commonsense reasoning for natural language processing.

6 Tutorial Abstract

Machine reasoning research aims to build interpretable AI systems that can solve problems or draw conclusions from what they are told (i.e. facts and observations) and already know (i.e. models, common sense and knowledge) under certain constraints. In this tutorial, we will (1) describe the motivation of this tutorial and give our definition on machine reasoning; (2) introduce typical machine reasoning frameworks, including symbolic reasoning, probabilistic reasoning, neural-symbolic reasoning and neural-evidence reasoning, and show their successful applications in real-world scenarios; (3) talk about the dilemma between black-box neural networks with state-of-the-art performance and machine reasoning approaches with better interpretability; (4) summarize the content of this tutorial and discuss possible future directions.

7 Presenters

Nan Duan is a Principal Researcher of the Natural Language Computing group at Microsoft Research Asia. His research focuses on question answering, semantic parsing, pre-trained models for learning joint representations of natural language and images/videos/codes/knowledge. His technologies have been widely used in Microsoft products like Bing, Ads, Chatbot, Azure, etc.

Duyu Tang is a Senior Researcher of the Natural Language Computing group at Microsoft Research Asia, working on natural language processing. Duyu's research has been advancing the state of art of robust, interpretable and trustworthy NLP systems, while making direct technical contributions to production. Over the years, Duyu worked on a wide range of NLP problems, from sentiment analysis, question answering, conversational semantic parsing, knowledge-driven machine reasoning, fact checking and fake news detection, to AI for software engineering. He has served as area chair for EMNLP 2020.

Ming Zhou Dr. Ming Zhou is Research Manager of the Natural Language Computing Group at Microsoft Research Asia and leads numerous research projects including next generation search engines, neural machine translation, machine reading comprehension, question-answering, chatbots, computer poetry, knowledge graph and recommendation systems. He has published over 200 papers at top conferences and journals. He has served as area chairs of ACL, EMNLP and many other conferences. He was ACL president in 2019.

References

Jacob Andreas, Jacob Rohrbach, Trevor Darrell, and Dan Klein. 2016. Neural module networks. In *CVPR*.

Dzmitry Bahdanau, Kyunghyun Cho, and Yoshua Bengio. 2014. Neural machine translation by jointly learning to align and translate. *arXiv preprint arXiv:1409.0473*.

Yoshua Bengio. 2019. The consciousness prior. In *arXiv*.

Tarek R. Besold, Artur S. d'Avila Garcez, Sebastian Bader, Howard Bowman, Pedro M. Domingos, Pascal Hitzler, Kai-Uwe Kühnberger, Luís C. Lamb, Daniel Lowd, Priscila Machado Vieira Lima, Leo de Penning, Gadi Pinkas, Hoifung Poon, and Gerson Zaverucha. 2017. Neural-symbolic learning and reasoning: A survey and interpretation. *CoRR*.

Antoine Bordes, Nicolas Usunier, and Alberto Garcia-Duran. 2013. Translating embeddings for modeling multi-relational data. In *NeurIPS*.

Léon Bottou. 2011. From machine learning to machine reasoning. In *arXiv*.

Danqi Chen and Wen-tau Yih. 2020. Open-domain question answering. In *Proceedings of the 58th Annual Meeting of the Association for Computational Linguistics: Tutorial Abstracts*, pages 34–37.

Xinyun Chen, Chen Liang, Adams Wei Yu, Denny Zhou, D. Song, and Quoc V. Le. 2020. Neural symbolic reader: Scalable integration of distributed and symbolic representations for reading comprehension. In *ICLR*.

Peter Clark, Oren Etzioni, Daniel Khashabi, Tushar Khot, Bhavana Dalvi Mishra, Kyle Richardson, Ashish Sabharwal, Carissa Schoenick, Oyvind Tafjord, Niket Tandon, et al. 2019. From'f'to'a'on the ny regents science exams: An overview of the aristo project. *arXiv preprint arXiv:1909.01958*.

Peter Clark, Oyvind Tafjord, and Kyle Richardson. 2020. Transformers as soft reasoners over language. *arXiv preprint arXiv:2002.05867*.

Tim Dettmers, Pasquale Minervini, Pontus Stenetorp, and Sebastian Riedel. 2018. Convolutional 2d knowledge graph embeddings. In *AAAI*.

Pedro Domingos and Matthew Richardson. 2004. Markov logic: A unifying framework for statistical relational learning.

Honghua Dong, Jiayuan Mao, Tian Lin, Chong Wang, Lihong Li, and Denny Zhou. 2019. Neural logic machines. In *ICLR*.

Li Dong and Mirella Lapata. 2016. Language to logical form with neural attention. In *ACL*.

Li Dong and Mirella Lapata. 2018. Coarse-to-fine decoding for neural semantic parsing. In *ACL*.

Xin Luna Dong, Evgeniy Gabrilovich, Geremy Heitz, Wilko Horn, Ni Lao, Kevin Murphy, Thomas Strohmann, Shaohua Sun, and Wei Zhang. 2014. Knowledge vault: A web-scale approach to probabilistic knowledge fusion. In *KDD*.

Mengnan Du, Ninghao Liu, and Xia Hu. 2020. Techniques for interpretable machine learning. *Communications of the ACM*.

Dheeru Dua, Yizhong Wang, Pradeep Dasigi, Gabriel Stanovsky, Sameer Singh, and Matt Gardner. 2019. Drop: A reading comprehension benchmark requiring discrete reasoning over paragraphs. *arXiv preprint arXiv:1903.00161*.

Artur d'Avila Garcez, Marco Gori, Luis C. Lamb, Luciano Serafini, Michael Spranger, and Son N. Tran. 2019. Neural-symbolic computing: An effective methodology for principled integration of machine learning and reasoning. *arXiv*.

Xavier Glorot, Antoine Bordes, Jason Weston, and Yoshua Bengio. 2013. A semantic matching energy function for learning with multi-relational data. In *arXiv*.

Daya Guo, Duyu Tang, Nan Duan, Ming Zhou, and Jian Yin. 2018. Dialog-to-action: Conversational question answering over a large-scale knowledge base. In *NeurIPS*.

Lingbing Guo, Zequn Sun, and Wei Hu. 2019. Learning to exploit long-term relational dependencies in knowledge graphs. In *ICML*.

Nitish Gupta, Kevin Lin, Dan Roth, Sameer Singh, and Matt Gardner. 2020. Neural module networks for reasoning over text. In *ICLR*.

Lisa Anne Hendricks, Zeynep Akata, Marcus Rohrbach, Jeff Donahue, Bernt Schiele, and Trevor Darrell. 2016. Generating visual explanations. In *European Conference on Computer Vision*, pages 3–19. Springer.

Ronghang Hu, Jacob Andreas, Marcus Rohrbach, Trevor Darrell, and Kate Saenko. 2017. Learning to reason: End-to-end module networks for visual question answering. In *ICCV*.

Zhiting Hu, Xuezhe Ma, Zhengzhong Liu, Eduard Hovy, and Eric Xing. 2016. Harnessing deep neural networks with logic rules. In *ACL*.

Komal K. Teru, Etienne Denis, and William L. Hamilton. 2020. Inductive relation prediction by subgraph reasoning. In *ICML*.

Roni Khardon and Dan Roth. 1994. Learning to reason. In *AAAI*.

Been Kim, Martin Wattenberg, Justin Gilmer, Carrie Cai, James Wexler, Fernanda Viegas, et al. 2018. Interpretability beyond feature attribution: Quantitative testing with concept activation vectors (tcav). In *International conference on machine learning*, pages 2668–2677. PMLR.

Tao Li and Vivek Srikumar. 2019. Augmenting neural networks with first-order logic. In *ACL*.

Yankai Lin, Zhiyuan Liu, Maosong Sun, Yang Liu, and Xuan Zhu. 2015. Learning entity and relation embeddings for knowledge graph completion. In *AAAI*.

Quan Liu, Hui Jiang, Andrew Evdokimov, Zhen-Hua Ling, Xiaodan Zhu, Si Wei, and Yu Hu. 2016. Probabilistic reasoning via deep learning: Neural association models. In *arXiv*.

Jiayuan Mao, Chuang Gan, Pushmeet Kohli, Joshua B. Tenenbaum, and Jiajun Wu. 2019. The neuro-symbolic concept learner: Interpreting scenes, words, and sentences from natural supervision. In *ICLR*.

John McCarthy. 1958. Program with common sense.

Judea Pearl. 1988. Probabilistic reasoning in intelligent systems: Networks of plausible inference. In *Morgan Kaufmann Publishers Inc.*

Meng Qu and Jian Tang. 2019. Probabilistic logic neural networks for reasoning. In *NeurIPS*.

Hannah Rashkin, Maarten Sap, Emily Allaway, Noah A Smith, and Yejin Choi. 2018. Event2mind: Commonsense inference on events, intents, and reactions. *arXiv preprint arXiv:1805.06939*.

Hongyu Ren, Weihua Hu, and Jure Leskovec. 2020. Query2box: Reasoning over knowledge graphs in vector space using box embeddings. In *ICLR*.

Marco Tulio Ribeiro, Sameer Singh, and Carlos Guestrin. 2016. " why should i trust you?" explaining the predictions of any classifier. In *Proceedings of the 22nd ACM SIGKDD international conference on knowledge discovery and data mining*, pages 1135–1144.

Matthew Richardson and Pedro Domingos. 2006. Markov logic networks. volume 62.

Tim Rocktaschel, Sameer Singh, and Sebastian Riedel. 2015. Injecting logical background knowledge into embeddings for relation extraction. In *NAACL*.

Tim Rocktäschel and Sebastian Riedel. 2017. End-to-end differentiable proving. In *NeurIPS*.

Maarten Sap, Ronan Le Bras, Emily Allaway, Chandra Bhagavatula, Nicholas Lourie, Hannah Rashkin, Brendan Roof, Noah A Smith, and Yejin Choi. 2019. Atomic: An atlas of machine commonsense for if-then reasoning. In *AAAI*.

Maarten Sap, Vered Shwartz, Antoine Bosselut, Yejin Choi, and Dan Roth. 2020. Commonsense reasoning for natural language processing. In *ACL*.

Karen Simonyan, Andrea Vedaldi, and Andrew Zisserman. 2013. Deep inside convolutional networks: Visualising image classification models and saliency maps. *arXiv preprint arXiv:1312.6034*.

Richard Socher, Danqi Chen, Christopher Manning, and Andrew Ng. 2013. Reasoning with neural tensor networks for knowledge base completion. In *NeurIPS*.

Shane Storks, Qiaozi Gao, and Joyce Y. Chai. 2019. Recent advances in natural language inference: A survey of benchmarks, resources, and approaches. *arXiv*.

Yibo Sun, Duyu Tang, Nan Duan, Jianshu Ji, Guihong Cao, Xiaocheng Feng, Bing Qin, Ting Liu, and Ming Zhou. 2018. Semantic parsing with syntax- and table-aware sql generation. In *ACL*.

Alon Talmor, Jonathan Herzig, Nicholas Lourie, and Jonathan Berant. 2019. Commonsenseqa: A question answering challenge targeting commonsense knowledge. *NAACL*.

James Thorne, Andreas Vlachos, Christos Christodoulopoulos, and Arpit Mittal. 2018. Fever: a large-scale dataset for fact extraction and verification. In *NAACL*.

Quan Wang, Zhendong Mao, Bin Wang, and Li Guo. 2017. Knowledge graph embedding: A survey of approaches and applications. In *IEEE-TKDE*.

Ruize Wang, Duyu Tang, Nan Duan, Wanjun Zhong, Zhongyu Wei, Xuanjing Huang, Daxin Jiang, and Ming Zhou. 2020. Leveraging declarative knowledge in text and first-order logic for fine-grained propaganda detection. In *EMNLP*.

Zhen Wang, Jianwen Zhang, Jianlin Feng, and Zheng Chen. 2014. Knowledge graph embedding by translating on hyperplanes. In *AAAI*.

Wenhan Xiong, Thien Hoang, and William Yang Wang. 2017. Deeppath: A reinforcement learning method for knowledge graph reasoning. In *EMNLP*.

Jingyi Xu, Zilu Zhang, Tal Friedman, Yitao Liang, and Guy Van den Broeck. 2018. A semantic loss function for deep learning with symbolic knowledge. In *ICML*.

Zhilin Yang, Peng Qi, Saizheng Zhang, Yoshua Bengio, William W Cohen, Ruslan Salakhutdinov, and Christopher D Manning. 2018. Hotpotqa: A dataset for diverse, explainable multi-hop question answering. *EMNLP*.

Weihao Yu, Zihang Jiang, Yanfei Dong, and Jiashi Feng. 2020. Reclor: A reading comprehension dataset requiring logical reasoning. *arXiv preprint arXiv:2002.04326*.

Quanshi Zhang, Ying Nian Wu, and Song-Chun Zhu. 2018. Interpretable convolutional neural networks. In *Proceedings of the IEEE Conference on Computer Vision and Pattern Recognition*, pages 8827–8836.

Victor Zhong, Mike Lewis, Sida I. Wang, and Luke Zettlemoyer. 2020. Grounded adaptation for zero-shot executable semantic parsing. In *EMNLP*.

Fact-Checking, Fake News, Propaganda, and Media Bias: Truth Seeking in the Post-Truth Era

Preslav Nakov
Qatar Computing Research Institute
Hamad Bin Khalifa University
pnakov@hbku.edu.qa

Giovanni Da San Martino
Department of Mathematics
University of Padova
dasan@math.unipd.it

1 Description

The rise of social media has democratized content creation and has made it easy for anybody to share and to spread information online. On the positive side, this has given rise to citizen journalism, thus enabling much faster dissemination of information compared to what was possible with newspapers, radio, and TV. On the negative side, stripping traditional media from their gate-keeping role has left the public unprotected against the spread of disinformation, which could now travel at breaking-news speed over the same democratic channel. This situation gave rise to the proliferation of false information specifically created to affect individual people's beliefs, and ultimately to influence major events such as political elections; it also set the dawn of the Post-Truth Era, where appeal to emotions has become more important than the truth. More recently, with the emergence of the COVID-19 pandemic, a new blending of medical and political misinformation and disinformation has given rise to the first global infodemic. Limiting the impact of these negative developments has become a major focus for journalists, social media companies, and regulatory authorities.

The tutorial offers an overview of the emerging and inter-connected research areas of fact-checking, misinformation, disinformation, "fake news", propaganda, and media bias detection, with focus on text and on computational approaches. It further explores the general fact-checking pipeline and important elements thereof such as check-worthiness estimation, spotting previous fact-checked claims, stance detection, source reliability estimation, and detecting malicious users in social media. Finally, it covers some recent developments such as the emergence of large-scale pre-trained language models, and the challenges and opportunities they offer.

2 Outline of the Tutorial

Here is an outline of the tutorial. More information and materials are available online.[1]

2.1 Introduction

(i) What is "fake news"?
   (a) definitions
   (b) properties

(ii) "Fake news" as a weapon of mass deception
   (a) impact on politics, finances, health
   (b) can we win the war on "fake news"?

2.2 Check-Worthiness

(i) Task definition

(ii) Datasets

(iii) Approaches
   (a) ClaimBuster
   (b) ClaimRank: modeling the context, multi-source learning, multi-linguality
   (c) CLEF shared tasks

2.3 Detecting Previously Fact-Checked Claims

(i) Task definition

(ii) Datasets, e.g., CLEF

(iii) Approaches

2.4 Fact-checking

(i) Task definitions

(ii) Datasets, e.g., Snopes, FEVER, ClamsKG, MultiFC

(iii) Information sources: knowledge bases, Wikipedia, Web, social media, multimedia, tables

[1] http://propaganda.qcri.org/emnlp20-tutorial

Proceedings of the 2020 Conference on Empirical Methods in Natural Language Processing: Tutorial Abstracts, pages 7–19
Online, November 19 - 20, 2020.
https://doi.org/10.18653/v1/P17

(iv) Tasks and approaches
  (a) fact-checking against knowledge bases
  (b) fact-checking against Wikipedia
  (c) fact-checking claims using the Web
  (d) fact-checking rumors in social media
  (e) fact-checking multi-modal claims, e.g., about images
  (f) fact-checking the answers in community question answering forums
(v) Shared tasks at SemEval and FEVER

2.5 Fake News Detection

(i) Task definitions
(ii) Datasets, e.g., FakeNewsNet, NELA-GT-2018
(iii) The language of fake news
(iv) Tasks and approaches

2.6 Stance Detection

(i) Task definitions and examples
(ii) Datasets
(iii) Stance detection as a key element of fact-checking
(iv) Information sources: text, social context, user profile
(v) Tasks and approaches
  (a) neural methods for stance detection
  (b) cross-language stance detection
(vi) Shared tasks at SemEval and the Fake News Challenge

2.7 Source Reliability and Media Bias Estimation

(i) Task definitions and examples
(ii) Datasets: Media Bias Fact/Check, AllSides, OpenSources, etc.
(iii) Source reliability as a key element of fact-checking
(iv) Special case: hyper-partisanship
(v) Information sources: article text, Wikipedia, social media
(vi) Tasks and approaches
  (a) neural methods for source reliability estimation
  (b) multi-modality
  (c) multi-task learning

2.8 Propaganda Detection

(i) Task definitions and examples
(ii) Propaganda techniques and examples
(iii) Datasets
(iv) Tasks and approaches

2.9 Malicious User Detection

(i) Typology of malicious users
(ii) Datasets
(iii) Tasks and approaches

2.10 Recent Developments and Future Challenges

(i) Deep fakes: images, voice, video, text
(ii) Text generation: GPT-2, GPT-3, GROVER
(iii) Defending against neural fake news
(iv) Fighting the COVID-19 Infodemic

3 Reading List

We recommend several surveys. Shu et al. (2017), which adopted a data mining perspective on "fake news" and focused on social media. Another survey (Zubiaga et al., 2018a) focused on rumor detection in social media. The survey by Thorne and Vlachos (2018) took a fact-checking perspective on "fake news" and related problems. The survey by Li et al. (2016) covering truth discovery in general. Lazer et al. (2018) offers a general overview and discussion on the science of "fake news", while Vosoughi et al. (2018) focuses on the process of proliferation of true and false news online. Other recent surveys focus on stance detection (Küçük and Can, 2020), on propaganda (Da San Martino et al., 2020b), on social bots (Ferrara et al., 2016), on false information (Zannettou et al., 2019b) and on bias on the Web (Baeza-Yates, 2018).

See also the list of references at the end.

4 Type of Tutorial

The tutorial is both introductory, covering a number of topics related to fact-checking, propaganda and disinformation, but it is also cutting-edge, covering some latest developments in these areas.

5 Prerequisites

Prior knowledge of natural language processing, machine learning, and deep learning would be needed in order to understand large parts of the contents of this tutorial.

6 Lecturers

6.1 Preslav Nakov

Dr. Preslav Nakov is a Principal Scientist at the Qatar Computing Research Institute (QCRI), HBKU. His research interests include computational linguistics, "fake news" detection, fact-checking, machine translation, question answering, sentiment analysis, lexical semantics, Web as a corpus, and biomedical text processing. He received his PhD degree from the University of California at Berkeley, and he was a Research Fellow in the National University of Singapore, a honorary lecturer in the Sofia University, and research staff at the Bulgarian Academy of Sciences.

At QCRI, he leads the Tanbih project,[2] developed in collaboration with MIT, which aims to limit the effect of "fake news", propaganda and media bias by making users aware of what they are reading. The project was featured by over 100 news outlets, including Forbes, Boston Globe, Aljazeera, MIT Technology Review, Science Daily, Popular Science, Fast Company, The Register, WIRED, and Engadget, among others.

As part of the project, he co-organized several shared tasks on fact-checking and propaganda detection at SemEval and CLEF, as well as a related NLP4IF workshop.

He is President of ACL SIGLEX, a Secretary of ACL SIGSLAV, and a member of the EACL advisory board. He is also member of the editorial board of TACL, CS&L, NLE, AI Communications, and Frontiers in AI, as well as of the Language Science Press Book Series on Phraseology and Multiword Expressions. He co-authored a Morgan & Claypool book on Semantic Relations between Nominals, two books on computer algorithms, and many research papers in top-tier conferences and journals. He received the Young Researcher Award at RANLP'2011, and he was the first to receive the Bulgarian President's John Atanasoff award, named after the inventor of the first automatic electronic digital computer.

[2]Tanbih project: `http://tanbih.qcri.org`

6.2 Giovanni Da San Martino

Giovanni Da San Martino is a Senior Assistant Professor at the University of Padova, Italy. His research interests are at the intersection of machine learning and natural language processing. He has been researching for 10+ years on these topics, publishing more than 60 publications in top-tier conferences and journals. He received his PhD from the University of Bologna, he was a Research Fellow at the University of Padova and a Scientist at Qatar Computing Research Institute. He has worked on several NLP tasks including paraphrase recognition, stance detection and community question answering. Currently, he is actively involved in researching on disinformation and propaganda detection. As part of this research he has been co-organiser of the Checkthat! labs at CLEF 2018-2020, the NLP4IF 2019-2020 workshops on "censorship, disinformation, and propaganda", the 2019 Hack the News Datathon and the SemEval-2020 task 11 on "Detection of propaganda techniques in news articles."

References

Aseel Addawood, Adam Badawy, Kristina Lerman, and Emilio Ferrara. 2019. Linguistic cues to deception: Identifying political trolls on social media. In *Proceedings of the International AAAI Conference on Web and Social Media*, ICWSM '19, pages 15–25, Munich, Germany.

Firoj Alam, Fahim Dalvi, Shaden Shaar, Nadir Durrani, Hamdy Mubarak, Alex Nikolov, Giovanni Da San Martino, Ahmed Abdelali, Hassan Sajjad, Kareem Darwish, and Preslav Nakov. 2020a. Fighting the COVID-19 infodemic in social media: A holistic perspective and a call to arms. *ArXiv preprint 2007.07996*.

Firoj Alam, Shaden Shaar, Fahim Dalvi, Hassan Sajjad, Alex Nikolov, Hamdy Mubarak, Giovanni Da San Martino, Ahmed Abdelali, Nadir Durrani, Kareem Darwish, and Preslav Nakov. 2020b. Fighting the COVID-19 infodemic: Modeling the perspective of journalists, fact-checkers, social media platforms, policy makers, and the society. *ArXiv preprint 2005.00033*.

Hunt Allcott and Matthew Gentzkow. 2017. Social media and fake news in the 2016 election. *Journal of Economic Perspectives*, 31(2):211–36.

Jisun An, Meeyoung Cha, Krishna Gummadi, Jon Crowcroft, and Daniele Quercia. 2012. Visualizing media bias through Twitter. In *Proceedings of the International AAAI Conference on Web and Social Media*, ICWSM '12, pages 2–5, Dublin, Ireland.

Atanas Atanasov, Gianmarco De Francisci Morales, and Preslav Nakov. 2019. Predicting the role of political trolls in social media. In *Proceedings of the 2019 SIGNLL Conference on Computational Natural Language Learning*, CoNLL '19, pages 1023–1034, Hong Kong, China.

Pepa Atanasova, Lluís Màrquez, Alberto Barrón-Cedeño, Tamer Elsayed, Reem Suwaileh, Wajdi Zaghouani, Spas Kyuchukov, Giovanni Da San Martino, and Preslav Nakov. 2018. Overview of the CLEF-2018 CheckThat! Lab on automatic identification and verification of political claims, Task 1: Check-worthiness. In *CLEF 2018 Working Notes. Working Notes of CLEF 2018 - Conference and Labs of the Evaluation Forum*, CEUR Workshop Proceedings, Avignon, France. CEUR-WS.org.

Pepa Atanasova, Preslav Nakov, Georgi Karadzhov, Mitra Mohtarami, and Giovanni Da San Martino. 2019a. Overview of the CLEF-2019 CheckThat! Lab on Automatic Identification and Verification of Claims. Task 1: Check-Worthiness. In *CLEF 2019 Working Notes. Working Notes of CLEF 2019 - Conference and Labs of the Evaluation Forum*, CEUR Workshop Proceedings, Lugano, Switzerland. CEUR-WS.org.

Pepa Atanasova, Preslav Nakov, Lluís Màrquez, Alberto Barrón-Cedeño, Georgi Karadzhov, Tsvetomila Mihaylova, Mitra Mohtarami, and James Glass. 2019b. Automatic fact-checking using context and discourse information. *J. Data and Information Quality*, 11(3):12:1–12:27.

Pepa Atanasova, Jakob Grue Simonsen, Christina Lioma, and Isabelle Augenstein. 2020. Generating fact checking explanations. In *Proceedings of the 58th Annual Meeting of the Association for Computational Linguistics*, ACL '20, pages 7352–7364.

Isabelle Augenstein, Christina Lioma, Dongsheng Wang, Lucas Chaves Lima, Casper Hansen, Christian Hansen, and Jakob Grue Simonsen. 2019. MultiFC: A real-world multi-domain dataset for evidence-based fact checking of claims. In *Proceedings of the 2019 Conference on Empirical Methods in Natural Language Processing and the 9th International Joint Conference on Natural Language Processing*, EMNLP-IJCNLP '19, pages 4685–4697, Hong Kong, China.

Mouhamadou Lamine Ba, Laure Berti-Equille, Kushal Shah, and Hossam M. Hammady. 2016. VERA: A platform for veracity estimation over web data. In *Proceedings of the 25th International Conference Companion on World Wide Web*, WWW '16, pages 159–162, Montréal, Québec, Canada.

Adam Badawy, Kristina Lerman, and Emilio Ferrara. 2019. Who falls for online political manipulation? In *Companion Proceedings of The 2019 World Wide Web Conference*, WWW '19, page 162–168, San Francisco, California, USA.

Ricardo Baeza-Yates. 2018. Bias on the web. *Commun. ACM*, 61(6):54–61.

Ramy Baly, Georgi Karadzhov, Dimitar Alexandrov, James Glass, and Preslav Nakov. 2018a. Predicting factuality of reporting and bias of news media sources. In *Proceedings of the 2018 Conference on Empirical Methods in Natural Language Processing*, EMNLP '18, pages 3528–3539, Brussels, Belgium.

Ramy Baly, Georgi Karadzhov, Jisun An, Haewoon Kwak, Yoan Dinkov, Ahmed Ali, James Glass, and Preslav Nakov. 2020. What was written vs. who read it: News media profiling using text analysis and social media context. In *Proceedings of the 58th Annual Meeting of the Association for Computational Linguistics*, ACL '20, pages 3364–3374.

Ramy Baly, Georgi Karadzhov, Abdelrhman Saleh, James Glass, and Preslav Nakov. 2019. Multi-task ordinal regression for jointly predicting the trustworthiness and the leading political ideology of news media. In *Proceedings of the 2019 Conference of the North American Chapter of the Association for Computational Linguistics: Human Language Technologies*, NAACL-HLT '19, pages 2109–2116, Minneapolis, Minnesota, USA.

Ramy Baly, Mitra Mohtarami, James Glass, Lluís Màrquez, Alessandro Moschitti, and Preslav Nakov. 2018b. Integrating stance detection and fact checking in a unified corpus. In *Proceedings of the 2018 Conference of the North American Chapter of the Association for Computational Linguistics: Human Language Technologies*, NAACL-HLT '18, pages 21–27, New Orleans, Louisiana, USA.

Alberto Barrón-Cedeño, Giovanni Da San Martino, Israa Jaradat, and Preslav Nakov. 2019. Proppy: Organizing the news based on their propagandistic content. *Information Processing & Management*, 56(5):1849 – 1864.

Alberto Barrón-Cedeño, Tamer Elsayed, Reem Suwaileh, Lluís Màrquez, Pepa Atanasova, Wajdi Zaghouani, Spas Kyuchukov, Giovanni Da San Martino, and Preslav Nakov. 2018. Overview of the CLEF-2018 CheckThat! Lab on automatic identification and verification of political claims, Task 2: Factuality. In *CLEF 2018 Working Notes. Working Notes of CLEF 2018 - Conference and Labs of the Evaluation Forum*, CEUR Workshop Proceedings, Avignon, France. CEUR-WS.org.

Alberto Barrón-Cedeño, Giovanni Da San Martino, Israa Jaradat, and Preslav Nakov. 2019. Proppy: A system to unmask propaganda in online news. In *Proceedings of the Thirty-Third AAAI Conference on Artificial Intelligence*, AAAI'19, pages 9847–9848, Honolulu, HI, USA.

Alberto Barrón-Cedeño, Tamer Elsayed, Preslav Nakov, Giovanni Da San Martino, Maram Hasanain, Reem Suwaileh, and Fatima Haouari. 2020. CheckThat! at CLEF 2020: Enabling the automatic identification and verification of claims in social media. In *Advances in Information Retrieval*, ECIR '20, pages 499–507, Lisbon, Portugal.

Alberto Barrón-Cedeño, Tamer Elsayed, Preslav Nakov, Giovanni Da San Martino, Maram Hasanain, Reem Suwaileh, Fatima Haouari, Nikolay Babulkov, Bayan Hamdan, Alex Nikolov, Shaden Shaar, and Zien Sheikh Ali. 2020. Overview of CheckThat! 2020 — automatic identification and verification of claims in social media. In *Proceedings of the 11th International Conference of the CLEF Association: Experimental IR Meets Multilinguality, Multimodality, and Interaction*, CLEF '2020, Thessaloniki, Greece.

Anya Belz. 2019. Fully automatic journalism: We need to talk about nonfake news generation. In *Proceedings of the First Conference on Truth and Trust Online*, TTO '19, London, United Kingdom.

Gillian Bolsover and Philip Howard. 2017. Computational propaganda and political big data: Moving toward a more critical research agenda. *Big Data*, 5(4):273–276.

Zhan Bu, Zhengyou Xia, and Jiandong Wang. 2013. A sock puppet detection algorithm on virtual spaces. *Know.-Based Syst.*, 37:366–377.

Ceren Budak, Sharad Goel, and Justin M Rao. 2016. Fair and balanced? Quantifying media bias through crowdsourced content analysis. *Public Opinion Quarterly*, 80(S1):250–271.

Kevin R. Canini, Bongwon Suh, and Peter L. Pirolli. 2011. Finding credible information sources in social networks based on content and social structure. In *Proceedings of the IEEE International Conference on Privacy, Security, Risk, and Trust, and the IEEE International Conference on Social Computing*, SocialCom/PASSAT '11, pages 1–8, Boston, Massachusetts, USA.

Carlos Castillo, Marcelo Mendoza, and Barbara Poblete. 2011. Information credibility on Twitter. In *Proceedings of the 20th International Conference on World Wide Web*, WWW '11, page 675–684, Hyderabad, India.

Carlos Castillo, Marcelo Mendoza, and Barbara Poblete. 2013. Predicting information credibility in time-sensitive social media. *Internet Research*, 23(5):560–588.

Abhijnan Chakraborty, Bhargavi Paranjape, Kakarla Kakarla, and Niloy Ganguly. 2016. Stop clickbait: Detecting and preventing clickbaits in online news media. In *Proceedings of the 2016 IEEE/ACM International Conference on Advances in Social Networks Analysis and Mining*, ASONAM '16, pages 9–16, San Francisco, California, USA.

Cheng Chen, Kui Wu, Venkatesh Srinivasan, and Xudong Zhang. 2013. Battling the Internet Water Army: detection of hidden paid posters. In *Proceedings of the 2013 IEEE/ACM International Conference on Advances in Social Networks Analysis and Mining*, ASONAM '13, pages 116–120, Niagara, Canada.

Sihao Chen, Daniel Khashabi, Wenpeng Yin, Chris Callison-Burch, and Dan Roth. 2019a. Seeing things from a different angle:discovering diverse perspectives about claims. In *Proceedings of the 2019 Conference of the North American Chapter of the Association for Computational Linguistics: Human Language Technologies*, NAACL-HLT '19, pages 542–557, Minneapolis, Minnesota, USA.

Wenhu Chen, Hongmin Wang, Jianshu Chen, Yunkai Zhang, Hong Wang, Shiyang Li, Xiyou Zhou, and William Yang Wang. 2019b. TabFact: A large-scale dataset for table-based fact verification. *arXiv preprint 1909.02164*.

Matteo Cinelli, Walter Quattrociocchi, Alessandro Galeazzi, Carlo Michele Valensise, Emanuele Brugnoli, Ana Lucia Schmidt, Paola Zola, Fabiana Zollo, and Antonio Scala. 2020. The COVID-19 social media infodemic. *arXiv preprint 2003.05004*.

Michael Conover, Jacob Ratkiewicz, Matthew R Francisco, Bruno Gonçalves, Filippo Menczer, and Alessandro Flammini. 2011. Political polarization on Twitter. In *Proceedings of the Fifth International AAAI Conference on Weblogs and Social Media*, ICWSM '11, pages 89–96, Barcelona, Spain.

Giovanni Da San Martino, Alberto Barrón-Cedeño, Henning Wachsmuth, Rostislav Petrov, and Preslav Nakov. 2020a. SemEval-2020 task 11: Detection of propaganda techniques in news articles. In *Proceedings of the International Workshop on Semantic Evaluation*, SemEval '20, Barcelona, Spain.

Giovanni Da San Martino, Alberto Barron-Cedeno, and Preslav Nakov. 2019a. Findings of the NLP4IF-2019 shared task on fine-grained propaganda detection. In *Proceedings of the 2nd Workshop on NLP for Internet Freedom (NLP4IF): Censorship, Disinformation, and Propaganda*, NLP4IFEMNLP '19, pages 162–170, Hong Kong, China.

Giovanni Da San Martino, Stefano Cresci, Alberto Barrón-Cedeño, Seunghak Yu, Roberto Di Pietro, and Preslav Nakov. 2020b. A survey on computational propaganda detection. In *Proceedings of the Twenty-Ninth International Joint Conference on Artificial Intelligence*, IJCAI-PRICAI '20, pages 4826–4832.

Giovanni Da San Martino, Shaden Shaar, Yifan Zhang, Seunghak Yu, Alberto Barrón-Cedeño, and Preslav Nakov. 2020. Prta: A system to support the analysis of propaganda techniques in the news. In *Proceedings of the 58th Annual Meeting of the Association for Computational Linguistics: System Demonstrations*, ACL '20, pages 287–293.

Giovanni Da San Martino, Seunghak Yu, Alberto Barron-Cedeno, Rostislav Petrov, and Preslav Nakov. 2019b. Fine-grained analysis of propaganda in news articles. In *Proceedings of the 2019 Conference on Empirical Methods in Natural Language Processing*, EMNLP '19, pages 5636–5646, Hong Kong, China.

Kareem Darwish, Dimitar Alexandrov, Preslav Nakov, and Yelena Mejova. 2017. Seminar users in the Arabic Twitter sphere. In *Proceedings of the 9th International Conference on Social Informatics*, SocInfo '17, pages 91–108, Oxford, UK.

Kareem Darwish, Michael Aupetit, Peter Stefanov, and Preslav Nakov. 2020. Unsupervised user stance detection on Twitter. In *Proceedings of the International AAAI Conference on Web and Social Media*, ICWSM '20, pages 141–152, Atlanta, Georgia, USA.

Sohan De Sarkar, Fan Yang, and Arjun Mukherjee. 2018. Attending sentences to detect satirical fake news. In *Proceedings of the 27th International Conference on Computational Linguistics*, COLING '18, pages 3371–3380, Santa Fe, New Mexico, USA.

Michela Del Vicario, Alessandro Bessi, Fabiana Zollo, Fabio Petroni, Antonio Scala, Guido Caldarelli, H Eugene Stanley, and Walter Quattrociocchi. 2016. The spreading of misinformation online. *Proceedings of the National Academy of Sciences*, 113(3):554–559.

Stefano DellaVigna and Ethan Kaplan. 2007. The Fox News effect: Media bias and voting. *The Quarterly Journal of Economics*, 122(3):1187–1234.

Leon Derczynski, Kalina Bontcheva, Maria Liakata, Rob Procter, Geraldine Wong Sak Hoi, and Arkaitz Zubiaga. 2017. SemEval-2017 Task 8: RumourEval: Determining rumour veracity and support for rumours. In *Proceedings of the 11th International Workshop on Semantic Evaluation*, SemEval '17, pages 60–67, Vancouver, Canada.

Yoan Dinkov, Ahmed Ali, Ivan Koychev, and Preslav Nakov. 2019a. Predicting the leading political ideology of YouTube channels using acoustic, textual, and metadata information. In *Proceedings of the 20th Annual Conference of the International Speech Communication Association*, INTERSPEECH '19, pages 501–505, Graz, Austria.

Yoan Dinkov, Ivan Koychev, and Preslav Nakov. 2019b. Detecting toxicity in news articles: Application to Bulgarian. In *Proceedings of the International Conference on Recent Advances in Natural Language Processing*, RANLP '19, pages 247–258.

Ming Dong, Bolong Zheng, Nguyen Quoc Viet Hung, Han Su, and Guohui Li. 2019. Multiple rumor source detection with graph convolutional networks. In *Proceedings of the 28th ACM International Conference on Information and Knowledge Management*, CIKM '19, page 569–578, Beijing, China.

Xin Luna Dong, Evgeniy Gabrilovich, Kevin Murphy, Van Dang, Wilko Horn, Camillo Lugaresi, Shaohua Sun, and Wei Zhang. 2015. Knowledge-based trust: Estimating the trustworthiness of web sources. *Proc. VLDB Endow.*, 8(9):938–949.

Sebastian Dungs, Ahmet Aker, Norbert Fuhr, and Kalina Bontcheva. 2018. Can rumour stance alone predict veracity? In *Proceedings of the 27th International Conference on Computational Linguistics*, COLING '18, pages 3360–3370, Santa Fe, New Mexico, USA.

Erick Elejalde, Leo Ferres, and Eelco Herder. 2018. On the nature of real and perceived bias in the mainstream media. *PloS one*, 13(3):e0193765.

Tamer Elsayed, Preslav Nakov, Alberto Barrón-Cedeño, Maram Hasanain, Reem Suwaileh, Pepa Atanasova, and Giovanni Da San Martino. 2019a. CheckThat! at CLEF 2019: Automatic identification and verification of claims. In *Proceedings of the 41st European Conference on Information Retrieval*, ECIR '19, pages 309–315, Cologne, Germany.

Tamer Elsayed, Preslav Nakov, Alberto Barrón-Cedeño, Maram Hasanain, Reem Suwaileh, Giovanni Da San Martino, and Pepa Atanasova. 2019b.

Overview of the CLEF-2019 CheckThat!: Automatic identification and verification of claims. In *Experimental IR Meets Multilinguality, Multimodality, and Interaction*, LNCS, Lugano, Switzerland. Springer.

Emilio Ferrara, Onur Varol, Clayton Davis, Filippo Menczer, and Alessandro Flammini. 2016. The rise of social bots. *Commun. ACM*, 59(7):96–104.

William Ferreira and Andreas Vlachos. 2016. Emergent: a novel data-set for stance classification. In *Proceedings of the 2016 Conference of the North American Chapter of the Association for Computational Linguistics: Human Language Technologies*, NAACL-HLT '16, pages 1163–1168, San Diego, California, USA.

Seth Flaxman, Sharad Goel, and Justin M Rao. 2016. Filter bubbles, echo chambers, and online news consumption. *Public opinion quarterly*, 80(S1):298–320.

Mohamed H. Gad-Elrab, Daria Stepanova, Jacopo Urbani, and Gerhard Weikum. 2019a. ExFaKT: A framework for explaining facts over knowledge graphs and text. In *Proceedings of the Twelfth ACM International Conference on Web Search and Data Mining*, WSDM '19, pages 87–95, Melbourne, Australia.

Mohamed H. Gad-Elrab, Daria Stepanova, Jacopo Urbani, and Gerhard Weikum. 2019b. Tracy: Tracing facts over knowledge graphs and text. In *The World Wide Web Conference*, WWW '19, pages 3516–3520, San Francisco, California, USA.

Kiran Garimella, Gianmarco De Francisci Morales, Aristides Gionis, and Michael Mathioudakis. 2018. Political discourse on social media: Echo chambers, gatekeepers, and the price of bipartisanship. In *Proceedings of the International World Wide Web Conference*, WWW '18, pages 913–922, Lyon, France.

Sebastian Gehrmann, Hendrik Strobelt, and Alexander Rush. 2019. GLTR: Statistical detection and visualization of generated text. In *Proceedings of the 57th Annual Meeting of the Association for Computational Linguistics: System Demonstrations*, ACL '19, pages 111–116, Florence, Italy.

Pepa Gencheva, Preslav Nakov, Lluís Màrquez, Alberto Barrón-Cedeño, and Ivan Koychev. 2017. A context-aware approach for detecting worth-checking claims in political debates. In *Proceedings of the International Conference on Recent Advances in Natural Language Processing*, RANLP '17, pages 267–276, Varna, Bulgaria.

Matthew Gentzkow and Jesse M Shapiro. 2006. Media bias and reputation. *Journal of political Economy*, 114(2):280–316.

Genevieve Gorrell, Ahmet Aker, Kalina Bontcheva, Leon Derczynski, Elena Kochkina, Maria Liakata, and Arkaitz Zubiaga. 2019. SemEval-2019 task 7: RumourEval, determining rumour veracity and support for rumours. In *Proceedings of the 13th International Workshop on Semantic Evaluation*, pages 845–854, Minneapolis, Minnesota, USA.

Tim Groseclose and Jeffrey Milyo. 2005. A measure of media bias. *The Quarterly Journal of Economics*, 120(4):1191–1237.

Ivan Habernal, Henning Wachsmuth, Iryna Gurevych, and Benno Stein. 2018. Before name-calling: Dynamics and triggers of ad hominem fallacies in web argumentation. In *Proceedings of the 2018 Conference of the North American Chapter of the Association for Computational Linguistics: Human Language Technologies*, NAACL-HLT '18, pages 386–396, New Orleans, Louisiana, USA.

Andreas Hanselowski, Avinesh PVS, Benjamin Schiller, Felix Caspelherr, Debanjan Chaudhuri, Christian M. Meyer, and Iryna Gurevych. 2018. A retrospective analysis of the fake news challenge stance-detection task. In *Proceedings of the 27th International Conference on Computational Linguistics*, COLING '18, pages 1859–1874, Santa Fe, New Mexico, USA.

Momchil Hardalov, Ivan Koychev, and Preslav Nakov. 2016. In search of credible news. In *Proceedings of the 17th International Conference on Artificial Intelligence: Methodology, Systems, and Applications*, AIMSA '16, pages 172–180, Varna, Bulgaria.

Maram Hasanain, Fatima Haouari, Reem Suwaileh, Zien Sheikh Ali, Bayan Hamdan, Tamer Elsayed, Alberto Barrón-Cedeño, Giovanni Da San Martino, and Preslav Nakov. 2020. Overview of the CLEF-2020 CheckThat! lab on automatic identification and verification of claims in social media: Arabic tasks. In *Working Notes of CLEF 2020—Conference and Labs of the Evaluation Forum*, CLEF '2020, Thessaloniki, Greece.

Maram Hasanain, Reem Suwaileh, Tamer Elsayed, Alberto Barrón-Cedeño, and Preslav Nakov. 2019. Overview of the CLEF-2019 CheckThat! Lab on Automatic Identification and Verification of Claims. Task 2: Evidence and Factuality. In *CLEF 2019 Working Notes. Working Notes of CLEF 2019 - Conference and Labs of the Evaluation Forum*, CEUR Workshop Proceedings, Lugano, Switzerland. CEUR-WS.org.

Naeemul Hassan, Chengkai Li, and Mark Tremayne. 2015. Detecting check-worthy factual claims in presidential debates. In *Proceedings of the 24th ACM International on Conference on Information and Knowledge Management*, CIKM '15, page 1835–1838, Melbourne, Australia.

Naeemul Hassan, Afroza Sultana, You Wu, Gensheng Zhang, Chengkai Li, Jun Yang, and Cong Yu. 2014. Data in, fact out: Automated monitoring of facts by FactWatcher. *PVLDB*, 7:1557–1560.

Naeemul Hassan, Gensheng Zhang, Fatma Arslan, Josue Caraballo, Damian Jimenez, Siddhant Gawsane, Shohedul Hasan, Minumol Joseph, Aaditya Kulkarni, Anil Kumar Nayak, Vikas Sable, Chengkai Li, and Mark Tremayne. 2017. ClaimBuster: The first-ever end-to-end fact-checking system. *Proc. VLDB Endow.*, 10(12):1945–1948.

Christopher Hidey, Tuhin Chakrabarty, Tariq Alhindi, Siddharth Varia, Kriste Krstovski, Mona Diab, and Smaranda Muresan. 2020. DeSePtion: Dual sequence prediction and adversarial examples for improved fact-checking. In *Proceedings of the 58th Annual Meeting of the Association for Computational Linguistics*, ACL '20, pages 8593–8606.

Renee Hobbs and Sandra Mcgee. 2008. Teaching about propaganda: An examination of the historical roots of media literacy. *Journal of Media Literacy Education*, 6(62):56–67.

Benjamin D. Horne, William Dron, Sara Khedr, and Sibel Adali. 2018a. Assessing the news landscape: A multi-module toolkit for evaluating the credibility of news. In *Proceedings of the The Web Conference*, WWW '18, pages 235–238, Lyon, France.

Benjamin D. Horne, Sara Khedr, and Sibel Adali. 2018b. Sampling the news producers: A large news and feature data set for the study of the complex media landscape. In *Proceedings of the Twelfth International Conference on Web and Social Media*, ICWSM '18, pages 518–527, Stanford, California, USA.

Benjamin D. Horne, Dorit Nevo, John O'Donovan, Jin-Hee Cho, and Sibel Adali. 2019a. Rating reliability and bias in news articles: Does AI assistance help everyone? In *Proceedings of the Thirteenth International Conference on Web and Social Media*, ICWSM '19, pages 247–256, Munich, Germany.

Benjamin D Horne, Jeppe Nørregaard, and Sibel Adalı. 2019b. Different spirals of sameness: A study of content sharing in mainstream and alternative media. In *Proceedings of the International AAAI Conference on Web and Social Media*, ICWSM '19, pages 257–266, Munich, Germany.

Viet-Phi Huynh and Paolo Papotti. 2019a. A benchmark for fact checking algorithms built on knowledge bases. In *Proceedings of the 28th ACM International Conference on Information and Knowledge Management*, CIKM '19, pages 689–698, Beijing, China.

Viet-Phi Huynh and Paolo Papotti. 2019b. A benchmark for fact checking algorithms built on knowledge bases. In *Proceedings of the 28th ACM International Conference on Information and Knowledge Management*, CIKM '19, page 689–698, Beijing, China.

Viet-Phi Huynh and Paolo Papotti. 2019c. Buckle: Evaluating fact checking algorithms built on knowledge bases. *Proc. VLDB Endow.*, 12(12):1798–1801.

Shanto Iyengar and Kyu S Hahn. 2009. Red media, blue media: Evidence of ideological selectivity in media use. *Journal of communication*, 59(1):19–39.

Israa Jaradat, Pepa Gencheva, Alberto Barrón-Cedeño, Lluís Màrquez, and Preslav Nakov. 2018. ClaimRank: Detecting check-worthy claims in Arabic and English. In *Proceedings of the 16th Annual Conference of the North American Chapter of the Association for Computational Linguistics: Human Language Technologies*, NAACL-HLT '18, pages 26–30, New Orleans, Louisiana, USA.

Shan Jiang, Miriam Metzger, Andrew Flanagin, and Christo Wilson. 2020. Modeling and measuring expressed (dis)belief in (mis)information. In *Proceedings of the International AAAI Conference on Web and Social Media*, ICWSM '20, pages 315–326, Atlanta, Georgia, USA.

Zhiwei Jin, Juan Cao, Yu-Gang Jiang, and Yongdong Zhang. 2014. News credibility evaluation on microblog with a hierarchical propagation model. In *Proceedings of the 2014 IEEE International Conference on Data Mining, ICDM 2014*, ICDM '14, pages 230–239, Shenzhen, China.

Zhiwei Jin, Juan Cao, Yongdong Zhang, and Jiebo Luo. 2016. News verification by exploiting conflicting social viewpoints in microblogs. In *Proceedings of the Thirtieth AAAI Conference on Artificial Intelligence*, AAAI '16, pages 2972–2978, Phoenix, AZ, USA.

Georgi Karadzhov, Pepa Gencheva, Preslav Nakov, and Ivan Koychev. 2017a. We built a fake news & click-bait filter: What happened next will blow your mind! In *Proceedings of the International Conference on Recent Advances in Natural Language Processing*, RANLP '17, pages 334–343, Varna, Bulgaria.

Georgi Karadzhov, Preslav Nakov, Lluís Màrquez, Alberto Barrón-Cedeño, and Ivan Koychev. 2017b. Fully automated fact checking using external sources. In *Proceedings of the International Conference on Recent Advances in Natural Language Processing*, RANLP '17, pages 344–353, Varna, Bulgaria.

Georgios Karagiannis, Immanuel Trummer, Saehan Jo, Shubham Khandelwal, Xuezhi Wang, and Cong Yu. 2019. Mining an "anti-knowledge base" from Wikipedia updates with applications to fact checking and beyond. *Proc. VLDB Endow.*, 13(4):561–573.

Twin Karmakharm, Nikolaos Aletras, and Kalina Bontcheva. 2019. Journalist-in-the-loop: Continuous learning as a service for rumour analysis. In *Proceedings of the 2019 Conference on Empirical Methods in Natural Language Processing and the 9th International Joint Conference on Natural Language Processing: System Demonstrations*,

EMNLP-IJCNLP '19, pages 115–120, Hong Kong, China.

Dhruv Khattar, Jaipal Singh Goud, Manish Gupta, and Vasudeva Varma. 2019. MVAE: Multimodal variational autoencoder for fake news detection. In *Proceedings of the World Wide Web Conference*, WWW '19, page 2915–2921, San Francisco, California, USA.

Johannes Kiesel, Maria Mestre, Rishabh Shukla, Emmanuel Vincent, Payam Adineh, David Corney, Benno Stein, and Martin Potthast. 2019. Semeval-2019 task 4: Hyperpartisan news detection. In *Proceedings of the 13th International Workshop on Semantic Evaluation*, SemEval '19, pages 829–839, Minneapolis, Minnesota, USA.

Elena Kochkina, Maria Liakata, and Arkaitz Zubiaga. 2018. All-in-one: Multi-task learning for rumour verification. In *Proceedings of the 27th International Conference on Computational Linguistics*, COLING '18, pages 3402–3413, Santa Fe, New Mexico, USA.

Lev Konstantinovskiy, Oliver Price, Mevan Babakar, and Arkaitz Zubiaga. 2018. Towards automated factchecking: Developing an annotation schema and benchmark for consistent automated claim detection. *ArXiv preprint 1809.08193.*

Daniel Kopev, Ahmed Ali, Ivan Koychev, and Preslav Nakov. 2019. Detecting deception in political debates using acoustic and textual features. In *Proceedings of the IEEE Automatic Speech Recognition and Understanding Workshop*, ASRU '19, pages 652–659, Singapore.

Dilek Küçük and Fazli Can. 2020. Stance detection: A survey. *ACM Comput. Surv.*, 53(1).

Vivek Kulkarni, Junting Ye, Steve Skiena, and William Yang Wang. 2018. Multi-view models for political ideology detection of news articles. In *Proceedings of the 2018 Conference on Empirical Methods in Natural Language Processing*, EMNLP '18, pages 3518–3527, Brussels, Belgium.

Srijan Kumar, Justin Cheng, Jure Leskovec, and V.S. Subrahmanian. 2017. An army of me: sockpuppets in online discussion communities. In *Proceedings of the 26th International Conference on World Wide Web*, WWW '17, pages 857–866, Perth, Australia.

Sejeong Kwon, Meeyoung Cha, and Kyomin Jung. 2017. Rumor detection over varying time windows. *PLoS ONE*, 12(1):e0168344.

Sejeong Kwon, Meeyoung Cha, Kyomin Jung, Wei Chen, and Yajun Wang. 2013. Prominent features of rumor propagation in online social media. In *Proceedings of the 13th IEEE International Conference on Data Mining*, ICDM '13, pages 1103–1108, Dallas, Texas, USA.

David M.J. Lazer, Matthew A. Baum, Yochai Benkler, Adam J. Berinsky, Kelly M. Greenhill, Filippo Menczer, Miriam J. Metzger, Brendan Nyhan, Gordon Pennycook, David Rothschild, Michael Schudson, Steven A. Sloman, Cass R. Sunstein, Emily A. Thorson, Duncan J. Watts, and Jonathan L. Zittrain. 2018. The science of fake news. *Science*, 359(6380):1094–1096.

Yaliang Li, Jing Gao, Chuishi Meng, Qi Li, Lu Su, Bo Zhao, Wei Fan, and Jiawei Han. 2016. A survey on truth discovery. *SIGKDD Explor. Newsl.*, 17(2):1–16.

Yang Liu and Yi-Fang Brook Wu. 2018. Early detection of fake news on social media through propagation path classification with recurrent and convolutional networks. In *Proceedings of the Thirty-Second AAAI Conference on Artificial Intelligence*, AAAI '18, pages 354–361, New Orleans, Louisiana, USA.

Yi-Ju Lu and Cheng-Te Li. 2020. GCAN: Graph-aware co-attention networks for explainable fake news detection on social media. In *Proceedings of the 58th Annual Meeting of the Association for Computational Linguistics*, ACL '20, pages 505–514.

Luca Luceri, Silvia Giordano, and Emilio Ferrara. 2020. Detecting troll behavior via inverse reinforcement learning: A case study of Russian trolls in the 2016 US election. In *Proceedings of the Fourteenth International AAAI Conference on Web and Social Media*, ICWSM '20, pages 417–427, Atlanta, Georgia, USA.

Michal Lukasik, Trevor Cohn, and Kalina Bontcheva. 2015. Point process modelling of rumour dynamics in social media. In *Proceedings of the 53rd Annual Meeting of the Association for Computational Linguistics and the 7th International Joint Conference on Natural Language Processing*, ACL-IJCNLP '15, pages 518–523, Beijing, China.

Jing Ma, Wei Gao, Prasenjit Mitra, Sejeong Kwon, Bernard J. Jansen, Kam-Fai Wong, and Meeyoung Cha. 2016. Detecting rumors from microblogs with recurrent neural networks. In *Proceedings of the Twenty-Fifth International Joint Conference on Artificial Intelligence*, IJCAI '16, pages 3818–3824, New York, NY, USA.

Jing Ma, Wei Gao, and Kam-Fai Wong. 2017. Detect rumors in microblog posts using propagation structure via kernel learning. In *Proceedings of the 55th Annual Meeting of the Association for Computational Linguistics*, ACL '17, pages 708–717, Vancouver, Canada.

Todor Mihaylov, Georgi Georgiev, and Preslav Nakov. 2015a. Finding opinion manipulation trolls in news community forums. In *Proceedings of the Nineteenth Conference on Computational Natural Language Learning*, CoNLL '15, pages 310–314, Beijing, China.

Todor Mihaylov, Ivan Koychev, Georgi Georgiev, and Preslav Nakov. 2015b. Exposing paid opinion manipulation trolls. In *Proceedings of the International Conference Recent Advances in Natural Language Processing*, RANLP '15, pages 443–450, Hissar, Bulgaria.

Todor Mihaylov, Tsvetomila Mihaylova, Preslav Nakov, Lluís Màrquez, Georgi Georgiev, and Ivan Koychev. 2018. The dark side of news community forums: Opinion manipulation trolls. *Internet Research*, 28(5):1292–1312.

Todor Mihaylov and Preslav Nakov. 2016. Hunting for troll comments in news community forums. In *Proceedings of the 54th Annual Meeting of the Association for Computational Linguistics*, ACL '16, pages 399–405, Berlin, Germany.

Tsvetomila Mihaylova, Georgi Karadzhov, Pepa Atanasova, Ramy Baly, Mitra Mohtarami, and Preslav Nakov. 2019. SemEval-2019 task 8: Fact checking in community question answering forums. In *Proceedings of the 13th International Workshop on Semantic Evaluation*, SemEval '19, pages 860–869, Minneapolis, Minnesota, USA.

Tsvetomila Mihaylova, Preslav Nakov, Lluís Màrquez, Alberto Barrón-Cedeño, Mitra Mohtarami, Georgi Karadjov, and James Glass. 2018. Fact checking in community forums. In *Proceedings of the Thirty-Second AAAI Conference on Artificial Intelligence*, AAAI '18, pages 5309–5316, New Orleans, Louisiana, USA.

Sebastião Miranda, David Nogueira, Afonso Mendes, Andreas Vlachos, Andrew Secker, Rebecca Garrett, Jeff Mitchel, and Zita Marinho. 2019. Automated fact checking in the news room. In *Proceedings of the World Wide Web Conference*, WWW '19, pages 3579–3583, San Francisco, California, USA.

Saif Mohammad, Svetlana Kiritchenko, Parinaz Sobhani, Xiaodan Zhu, and Colin Cherry. 2016. SemEval-2016 task 6: Detecting stance in tweets. In *Proceedings of the 10th International Workshop on Semantic Evaluation*, SemEval '16, pages 31–41, San Diego, California, USA.

Mitra Mohtarami, Ramy Baly, James Glass, Preslav Nakov, Lluís Màrquez, and Alessandro Moschitti. 2018. Automatic stance detection using end-to-end memory networks. In *Proceedings of the 16th Annual Conference of the North American Chapter of the Association for Computational Linguistics: Human Language Technologies*, NAACL-HLT '18, pages 767–776, New Orleans, Louisiana, USA.

Mitra Mohtarami, James Glass, and Preslav Nakov. 2019. Contrastive language adaptation for cross-lingual stance detection. In *Proceedings of the 2019 Conference on Empirical Methods in Natural Language Processing*, EMNLP '19, pages 4442–4452, Hong Kong, China.

Meredith Ringel Morris, Scott Counts, Asta Roseway, Aaron Hoff, and Julia Schwarz. 2012. Tweeting is believing?: Understanding microblog credibility perceptions. In *Proceedings of the ACM 2012 Conference on Computer Supported Cooperative Work*, CSCW '12, pages 441–450, Seattle, Washington, USA.

Subhabrata Mukherjee and Gerhard Weikum. 2015. Leveraging joint interactions for credibility analysis in news communities. In *Proceedings of the 24th ACM International on Conference on Information and Knowledge Management*, CIKM '15, pages 353–362, Melbourne, Australia.

Moin Nadeem, Wei Fang, Brian Xu, Mitra Mohtarami, and James Glass. 2019. FAKTA: An automatic end-to-end fact checking system. In *Proceedings of the 2019 Conference of the North American Chapter of the Association for Computational Linguistics*, NAACL-HLT '19, pages 78–83, Minneapolis, Minnesota, USA.

Preslav Nakov. 2020. Can we spot the "fake news" before it was even written? *arXiv preprint 2008.04374*.

Preslav Nakov, Alberto Barrón-Cedeño, Tamer Elsayed, Reem Suwaileh, Lluís Màrquez, Wajdi Zaghouani, Pepa Atanasova, Spas Kyuchukov, and Giovanni Da San Martino. 2018. Overview of the CLEF-2018 CheckThat! Lab on automatic identification and verification of political claims. In *Proceedings of the Ninth International Conference of the CLEF Association: Experimental IR Meets Multilinguality, Multimodality, and Interaction*, Lecture Notes in Computer Science, pages 372–387, Avignon, France. Springer.

Preslav Nakov, Tsvetomila Mihaylova, Lluís Màrquez, Yashkumar Shiroya, and Ivan Koychev. 2017. Do not trust the trolls: Predicting credibility in community question answering forums. In *Proceedings of the International Conference on Recent Advances in Natural Language Processing*, RANLP '17, pages 551–560, Varna, Bulgaria.

An T. Nguyen, Aditya Kharosekar, Matthew Lease, and Byron C. Wallace. 2018. An interpretable joint graphical model for fact-checking from crowds. In *Proceedings of the Thirty-Second AAAI Conference on Artificial Intelligence*, AAAI '18, New Orleans, Louisiana, USA.

Van-Hoang Nguyen, Kazunari Sugiyama, Preslav Nakov, and Min-Yen Kan. 2020. FANG: Leveraging social context for fake news detection using graph representation. In *Proceedings of the 29th ACM International Conference on Information and Knowledge Management*, CIKM '20.

Yixin Nie, Haonan Chen, and Mohit Bansal. 2019. Combining fact extraction and verification with neural semantic matching networks. In *Proceedings of the Thirty-Third AAAI Conference on Artificial Intelligence*, AAAI '19, pages 6859–6866, Honolulu, Hawaii, USA.

Jeppe Nørregaard, Benjamin D. Horne, and Sibel Adali. 2019. NELA-GT-2018: A large multi-labelled news dataset for the study of misinformation in news articles. In *Proceedings of the Thirteenth International Conference on Web and Social Media*, ICWSM '19, pages 630–638, Munich, Germany.

Symeon Papadopoulos, Kalina Bontcheva, Eva Jaho, Mihai Lupu, and Carlos Castillo. 2016. Overview of the special issue on trust and veracity of information in social media. *ACM Trans. Inf. Syst.*, 34(3):14:1–14:5.

Verónica Pérez-Rosas, Bennett Kleinberg, Alexandra Lefevre, and Rada Mihalcea. 2018. Automatic detection of fake news. In *Proceedings of the 27th International Conference on Computational Linguistics*, COLING '18, pages 3391–3401, Santa Fe, New Mexico, USA.

Evaggelia Pitoura, Panayiotis Tsaparas, Giorgos Flouris, Irini Fundulaki, Panagiotis Papadakos, Serge Abiteboul, and Gerhard Weikum. 2018. On measuring bias in online information. *SIGMOD Rec.*, 46(4):16–21.

Kashyap Popat, Subhabrata Mukherjee, Jannik Strötgen, and Gerhard Weikum. 2016. Credibility assessment of textual claims on the web. In *Proceedings of the 25th ACM International Conference on Information and Knowledge Management*, CIKM '16, pages 2173–2178, Indianapolis, Indiana, USA.

Kashyap Popat, Subhabrata Mukherjee, Jannik Strötgen, and Gerhard Weikum. 2017. Where the truth lies: Explaining the credibility of emerging claims on the Web and social media. In *Proceedings of the 26th International Conference on World Wide Web Companion*, WWW '17, pages 1003–1012, Perth, Australia.

Kashyap Popat, Subhabrata Mukherjee, Jannik Strötgen, and Gerhard Weikum. 2018. CredEye: A credibility lens for analyzing and explaining misinformation. In *Proceedings of The Web Conference 2018*, WWW '18, pages 155–158, Lyon, France.

Martin Potthast, Johannes Kiesel, Kevin Reinartz, Janek Bevendorff, and Benno Stein. 2018. A stylometric inquiry into hyperpartisan and fake news. In *Proceedings of the 56th Annual Meeting of the Association for Computational Linguistics*, ACL '18, pages 231–240, Melbourne, Australia.

Hannah Rashkin, Eunsol Choi, Jin Yea Jang, Svitlana Volkova, and Yejin Choi. 2017. Truth of varying shades: Analyzing language in fake news and political fact-checking. In *Proceedings of the 2017 Conference on Empirical Methods in Natural Language Processing*, EMNLP '17, pages 2931–2937, Copenhagen, Denmark.

Jacob Ratkiewicz, Michael Conover, Mark Meiss, Bruno Gonçalves, Snehal Patil, Alessandro Flammini, and Filippo Menczer. 2011. Truthy: Mapping the spread of astroturf in microblog streams. In *Proceedings of the 20th International Conference Companion on World Wide Web*, WWW '11, pages 249–252, Hyderabad, India.

Marta Recasens, Cristian Danescu-Niculescu-Mizil, and Dan Jurafsky. 2013. Linguistic models for analyzing and detecting biased language. In *Proceedings of the 51st Annual Meeting of the Association for Computational Linguistics*, ACL '13, pages 1650–1659, Sofia, Bulgaria.

Filipe N Ribeiro, Lucas Henrique, Fabricio Benevenuto, Abhijnan Chakraborty, Juhi Kulshrestha, Mahmoudreza Babaei, and Krishna P Gummadi. 2018. Media bias monitor: Quantifying biases of social media news outlets at large-scale. In *Proceedings of the Twelfth International AAAI Conference on Web and Social Media*, ICWSM '18, pages 290–299, Stanford, California, USA.

Benjamin Riedel, Isabelle Augenstein, Georgios P Spithourakis, and Sebastian Riedel. 2017. A simple but tough-to-beat baseline for the Fake News Challenge stance detection task. *ArXiv preprint 1707.03264*.

Natali Ruchansky, Sungyong Seo, and Yan Liu. 2017. CSI: A hybrid deep model for fake news detection. In *Proceedings of the 2017 ACM on Conference on Information and Knowledge Management*, CIKM '17, page 797–806, Singapore.

Diego Saez-Trumper, Carlos Castillo, and Mounia Lalmas. 2013. Social media news communities: Gatekeeping, coverage, and statement bias. In *Proceedings of the 22nd ACM International Conference on Information & Knowledge Management*, CIKM '13, pages 1679–1684, San Francisco, California, USA.

Shaden Shaar, Nikolay Babulkov, Giovanni Da San Martino, and Preslav Nakov. 2020a. That is a known lie: Detecting previously fact-checked claims. In *Proceedings of the 58th Annual Meeting of the Association for Computational Linguistics*, ACL '20, pages 3607–3618.

Shaden Shaar, Alex Nikolov, Nikolay Babulkov, Firoj Alam, Alberto Barrón-Cedeño, Tamer Elsayed, Maram Hasanain, Reem Suwaileh, Fatima Haouari, Giovanni Da San Martino, and Preslav Nakov. 2020b. Overview of the CLEF-2020 CheckThat! lab on automatic identification and verification of claims in social media: English tasks. In *Working Notes of CLEF 2020—Conference and Labs of the Evaluation Forum*, CLEF '2020, Thessaloniki, Greece.

Gautam Kishore Shahi, Anne Dirkson, and Tim A. Majchrzak. 2020. An exploratory study of COVID-19 misinformation on Twitter. *ArXiv preprint 2005.05710*.

Chengcheng Shao, Giovanni Luca Ciampaglia, Alessandro Flammini, and Filippo Menczer. 2016. Hoaxy: A platform for tracking online misinformation. In *Proceedings of the 25th International Conference Companion on World Wide Web*, WWW '16 Companion, pages 745–750, Geneva, Switzerland.

Prashant Shiralkar, Alessandro Flammini, Filippo Menczer, and Giovanni Luca Ciampaglia. 2017. Finding streams in knowledge graphs to support fact checking. In *Proceedings of the IEEE International Conference on Data Mining*, ICDM '17, New Orleans, Louisiana, USA.

Kai Shu, Deepak Mahudeswaran, Suhang Wang, Dongwon Lee, and Huan Liu. 2018. FakeNewsNet: A data repository with news content, social context and dynamic information for studying fake news on social media. *arXiv preprint arXiv:1809.01286*.

Kai Shu, Amy Sliva, Suhang Wang, Jiliang Tang, and Huan Liu. 2017. Fake news detection on social media: A data mining perspective. *SIGKDD Explor. Newsl.*, 19(1):22–36.

Kai Shu, Suhang Wang, and Huan Liu. 2019. Beyond news contents: The role of social context for fake news detection. In *Proceedings of the 12th ACM International Conference on Web Search and Data Mining*, WSDM '19, pages 312–320, Melbourne, Australia.

Peter Stefanov, Kareem Darwish, Atanas Atanasov, and Preslav Nakov. 2020. Predicting the topical stance and political leaning of media using tweets. In *Proceedings of the 58th Annual Meeting of the Association for Computational Linguistics*, ACL '20, pages 527–537.

Edson C. Tandoc Jr., Zheng Wei Lim, and Richard Ling. 2018. Defining "fake news". *Digital Journalism*, 6(2):137–153.

Andon Tchechmedjiev, Pavlos Fafalios, Katarina Boland, Malo Gasquet, Matthäus Zloch, Benjamin Zapilko, Stefan Dietze, and Konstantin Todorov. 2019. ClaimsKG: A knowledge graph of fact-checked claims. In *Proceedings of the 18th International Semantic Web Conference*, ISWC '19, pages 309–324, Auckland, New Zealand.

Denis Teyssou, Jean-Michel Leung, Evlampios Apostolidis, Konstantinos Apostolidis, Symeon Papadopoulos, Markos Zampoglou, Olga Papadopoulou, and Vasileios Mezaris. 2017. The InVID plug-in: Web video verification on the browser. In *Proceedings of the First International Workshop on Multimedia Verification*, MuVer '17, pages 23—30, Mountain View, California, USA.

James Thorne, Mingjie Chen, Giorgos Myrianthous, Jiashu Pu, Xiaoxuan Wang, and Andreas Vlachos. 2017. Fake news stance detection using stacked ensemble of classifiers. In *Proceedings of the EMNLP Workshop on Natural Language Processing meets Journalism*, pages 80–83, Copenhagen, Denmark.

James Thorne and Andreas Vlachos. 2018. Automated fact checking: Task formulations, methods and future directions. In *Proceedings of the 27th International Conference on Computational Linguistics*, COLING '18, pages 3346–3359, Santa Fe, New Mexico, USA.

James Thorne, Andreas Vlachos, Christos Christodoulopoulos, and Arpit Mittal. 2018a. FEVER: a large-scale dataset for fact extraction and VERification. In *Proceedings of the 2018 Conference of the North American Chapter of the Association for Computational Linguistics: Human Language Technologies*, NAACL-HLT '18, pages 809–819, New Orleans, Louisiana, USA.

James Thorne, Andreas Vlachos, Christos Christodoulopoulos, and Arpit Mittal. 2019a. Evaluating adversarial attacks against multiple fact verification systems. In *Proceedings of the 2019 Conference on Empirical Methods in Natural Language Processing and the 9th International Joint Conference on Natural Language Processing*, EMNLP-IJCNLP '19, pages 2944–2953, Hong Kong, China.

James Thorne, Andreas Vlachos, Oana Cocarascu, Christos Christodoulopoulos, and Arpit Mittal. 2018b. The fact extraction and VERification (FEVER) shared task. In *Proceedings of the First Workshop on Fact Extraction and VERification*, FEVER '18, pages 1–9, Brussels, Belgium.

James Thorne, Andreas Vlachos, Oana Cocarascu, Christos Christodoulopoulos, and Arpit Mittal. 2019b. The FEVER2.0 shared task. In *Proceedings of the Second Workshop on Fact Extraction and VERification*, FEVER '19, pages 1–6, Hong Kong, China.

Onur Varol, Emilio Ferrara, Clayton A. Davis, Filippo Menczer, and Alessandro Flammini. 2017. Online human-bot interactions: Detection, estimation, and characterization. In *Proceedings of the Eleventh International Conference on Web and Social Media*, ICWSM '17, pages 280–289, Montréal, Québec, Canada.

Slavena Vasileva, Pepa Atanasova, Lluís Màrquez, Alberto Barrón-Cedeño, and Preslav Nakov. 2019. It takes nine to smell a rat: Neural multi-task learning for check-worthiness prediction. In *Proceedings of the International Conference on Recent Advances in Natural Language Processing*, RANLP '19, pages 1229–1239, Varna, Bulgaria.

Andreas Vlachos and Sebastian Riedel. 2014. Fact checking: Task definition and dataset construction. In *Proceedings of the ACL 2014 Workshop on Language Technologies and Computational Social Science*, pages 18–22, Baltimore, Maryland, USA.

Soroush Vosoughi, Deb Roy, and Sinan Aral. 2018. The spread of true and false news online. *Science*, 359(6380):1146–1151.

William Yang Wang. 2017. "Liar, Liar Pants on Fire": A new benchmark dataset for fake news detection. In *Proceedings of the 55th Annual Meeting of the Association for Computational Linguistics*, ACL '17, pages 422–426, Vancouver, Canada.

Yaqing Wang, Fenglong Ma, Zhiwei Jin, Ye Yuan, Guangxu Xun, Kishlay Jha, Lu Su, and Jing Gao. 2018. EANN: Event adversarial neural networks for multi-modal fake news detection. In *Proceedings of the 24th ACM SIGKDD International Conference on Knowledge Discovery amp; Data Mining*, KDD '18, page 849–857, London, United Kingdom.

Lianwei Wu, Yuan Rao, Yongqiang Zhao, Hao Liang, and Ambreen Nazir. 2020. DTCA: Decision tree-based co-attention networks for explainable claim verification. In *Proceedings of the 58th Annual Meeting of the Association for Computational Linguistics*, ACL '20, pages 1024–1035.

You Wu, Pankaj K. Agarwal, Chengkai Li, Jun Yang, and Cong Yu. 2017. Computational fact checking through query perturbations. *ACM Trans. Database Syst.*, 42(1).

Kai-Cheng Yang, Onur Varol, Clayton A. Davis, Emilio Ferrara, Alessandro Flammini, and Filippo Menczer. 2019. Arming the public with artificial intelligence to counter social bots. *Human Behavior and Emerging Technologies*, 1(1):48–61.

Kai-Cheng Yang, Onur Varol, Pik-Mai Hui, and Filippo Menczer. 2020. Scalable and generalizable social bot detection through data selection. In *Proceedings of the Thirty-Fourth AAAI Conference on Artificial Intelligence*, AAAI '20, pages 1096–1103, New York, New York, USA.

Savvas Zannettou, Tristan Caulfield, Emiliano De Cristofaro, Michael Sirivianos, Gianluca Stringhini, and Jeremy Blackburn. 2019a. Disinformation warfare: Understanding state-sponsored trolls on Twitter and their influence on the web. In *Companion Proceedings of The 2019 World Wide Web Conference*, WWW '19, page 218–226, San Francisco, California, USA.

Savvas Zannettou, Michael Sirivianos, Jeremy Blackburn, and Nicolas Kourtellis. 2019b. The web of false information: Rumors, fake news, hoaxes, clickbait, and various other shenanigans. *J. Data and Information Quality*, 11(3):10:1–10:37.

Rowan Zellers, Ari Holtzman, Hannah Rashkin, Yonatan Bisk, Ali Farhadi, Franziska Roesner, and Yejin Choi. 2019. Defending against neural fake news. In *Advances in Neural Information Processing Systems 32*, NeurIPS '19, pages 9054–9065, Vancouver, Canada.

Amy X. Zhang, Aditya Ranganathan, Sarah Emlen Metz, Scott Appling, Connie Moon Sehat, Norman Gilmore, Nick B. Adams, Emmanuel Vincent, Jennifer Lee, Martin Robbins, Ed Bice, Sandro Hawke, David R. Karger, and An Xiao Mina. 2018. A structured response to misinformation: Defining and annotating credibility indicators in news articles. In *Proceedings of the The Web Conference*, WWW '18 companion, pages 603–612, Lyon, France.

Yifan Zhang, Giovanni Da San Martino, Alberto Barrón-Cedeño, Salvatore Romeo, Jisun An, Haewoon Kwak, Todor Staykovski, Israa Jaradat, Georgi Karadzhov, Ramy Baly, Kareem Darwish, and Preslav Nakov James Glass. 2019. Tanbih: Get to know what you are reading. In *Proceedings of the 2019 Conference on Empirical Methods in Natural Language Processing*, EMNLP '19, pages 223–228, Hong Kong, China.

Wanjun Zhong, Jingjing Xu, Duyu Tang, Zenan Xu, Nan Duan, Ming Zhou, Jiahai Wang, and Jian Yin. 2020. Reasoning over semantic-level graph for fact checking. In *Proceedings of the 58th Annual Meeting of the Association for Computational Linguistics*, ACL '20, pages 6170–6180, Online.

Xinyi Zhou, Apurva Mulay, Emilio Ferrara, and Reza Zafarani. 2020. ReCOVery: A multimodal repository for COVID-19 news credibility research. *arXiv preprint 2006.05557*.

Dimitrina Zlatkova, Preslav Nakov, and Ivan Koychev. 2019. Fact-checking meets fauxtography: Verifying claims about images. In *Proceedings of the Conference on Empirical Methods in Natural Language Processing*, EMNLP '19, pages 2099–2108, Hong Kong, China.

Arkaitz Zubiaga, Ahmet Aker, Kalina Bontcheva, Maria Liakata, and Rob Procter. 2018a. Detection and resolution of rumours in social media: A survey. *ACM Comput. Surv.*, 51(2).

Arkaitz Zubiaga and Heng Ji. 2014. Tweet, but verify: epistemic study of information verification on Twitter. *Social Network Analysis and Mining*, 4(1):1–12.

Arkaitz Zubiaga, Elena Kochkina, Maria Liakata, Rob Procter, Michal Lukasik, Kalina Bontcheva, Trevor Cohn, and Isabelle Augenstein. 2018b. Discourse-aware rumour stance classification in social media using sequential classifiers. *Inf. Process. Manage.*, 54(2):273–290.

Arkaitz Zubiaga, Maria Liakata, Rob Procter, Geraldine Wong Sak Hoi, and Peter Tolmie. 2016. Analysing how people orient to and spread rumours in social media by looking at conversational threads. *PLoS ONE*, 11(3):1–29.

Interpreting Predictions of NLP Models

Eric Wallace
UC Berkeley
ericwallace@berkeley.edu

Matt Gardner
Allen Institute for AI
mattg@allenai.org

Sameer Singh
UC Irvine
sameer@uci.edu

Abstract

Although neural NLP models are highly expressive and empirically successful, they also systematically fail in counterintuitive ways and are opaque in their decision-making process. This tutorial will provide a background on interpretation techniques, i.e., methods for explaining the predictions of NLP models. We will first situate *example-specific* interpretations in the context of other ways to understand models (e.g., probing, dataset analyses). Next, we will present a thorough study of example-specific interpretations, including saliency maps, input perturbations (e.g., LIME, input reduction), adversarial attacks, and influence functions. Alongside these descriptions, we will walk through source code that creates and visualizes interpretations for a diverse set of NLP tasks. Finally, we will discuss open problems in the field, e.g., evaluating, extending, and improving interpretation methods. The tutorial slides and the accompanying code is available online at https://www.ericswallace.com/interpretability.

1 Tutorial Description

Neural models have become the de-facto standard tool for NLP tasks. These models are becoming increasingly powerful—recent work shows that large neural models substantially improve accuracy on a wide range of downstream tasks (Devlin et al., 2019; Brown et al., 2020). However, today's models still make egregious errors: they reinforce racial biases (Sap et al., 2019), fail in counterintuitive ways (Jia and Liang, 2017; Feng et al., 2018), and often solve tasks using simple surface-level patterns (Gururangan et al., 2018; Min et al., 2019).

These model insufficiencies are exacerbated by the inability to understand *why* models made the predictions they do. Interpretation methods seek to fill this void. In particular, *example-specific* interpretations provide post-hoc explanations for individual model predictions. These explanations come in various forms, e.g., attributing the importance of the input features through saliency maps (Smilkov et al., 2017), perturbing the inputs and observing the model's response (Feng et al., 2018; Ribeiro et al., 2018b), or locating a model's local decision boundary (Ribeiro et al., 2016).

This tutorial will provide an introduction to the various types of example-specific interpretations. We will present the technical details of existing methods, including saliency maps, adversarial attacks, input perturbations, influence functions, and other methods. We will cover how these interpretations are applied to various tasks and input-output formats, e.g., text classification using LSTMs, masked language modeling using BERT (Devlin et al., 2019), and text generation using GPT-2 (Radford et al., 2019).

For each task, we will walk through example use cases of interpretations: highlighting model weaknesses (Jia and Liang, 2017), increasing/decreasing user trust (Feng et al., 2018), and understanding hard-to-formalize criteria such as bias, safety, and fairness (Doshi-Velez and Kim, 2017). Alongside the tutorial, we will present source code implementations of various interpretation methods using AllenNLP Interpret (Wallace et al., 2019b).

2 Details and Prerequisites

The tutorial will be of the *cutting-edge* type. The tutorial slides and the accompanying code is available online at https://www.ericswallace.com/interpretability.

Prerequisites Attendees should have a basic understanding of different tasks in NLP such as text classification, sequence tagging, and reading comprehension (predicting spans in a passage).

Attendees should also have a basic understanding of neural network methods for NLP, including:

Proceedings of the 2020 Conference on Empirical Methods in Natural Language Processing: Tutorial Abstracts, pages 20–23
Online, November 19 - 20, 2020. ©2020 Association for Computational Linguistics
https://doi.org/10.18653/v1/P17

- How backpropagation can compute gradients with respect to the parameters.
- How tokens/words are represented (i.e., word and sub-word embeddings).
- High-level ideas behind different model architectures (e.g., RNNs, Transformers).
- Optional knowledge of contextualized embedding models such as ELMo (Peters et al., 2018) and BERT (Devlin et al., 2019).

Finally, a portion of the tutorial will walk through Python code samples in PyTorch and AllenNLP (Gardner et al., 2018b). Participants do not need to understand this code to follow the main tutorial material.

Reading List Doshi-Velez and Kim (2017) provide a great overview and motivation for interpretability research. Lipton (2018) and Jain and Wallace (2019) discuss some of the challenges of defining and evaluating interpretability. Jia and Liang (2017) help demonstrate the fragility of NLP models. LIME (Ribeiro et al., 2016) and saliency maps (Simonyan et al., 2014) are now standard interpretations. Wallace et al. (2019b) provides example NLP interpretations (interested readers can inspect their code).

3 Tutorial Outline

The tutorial will present three hours of content with a thirty-minute break.

Motivation This section will discuss why we care about interpretability. It will paint a landscape of today's neural models, describe how models are brittle and behave counterintuitively, and explain how interpretations can open the "black box" of machine learning.

Introduction to Interpretations This section will situate *example-specific* interpretations in the context of other methods. We will discuss:

- Dataset analyses, e.g., error analysis, Errudite (Wu et al., 2019), diagnostic "challenge" test sets (Naik et al., 2018; Gardner et al., 2020)
- "Probing", i.e., inspecting a model's embeddings for certain properties (Liu et al., 2019; Tenney et al., 2019).
- Rationale-based explanations, i.e., a model generates text for why it made its prediction.
- Example-specific interpretations (our tutorial's focus), e.g., saliency maps (Simonyan et al., 2014), LIME (Ribeiro et al., 2016), adversarial attacks (Szegedy et al., 2014), and input perturbations (Feng et al., 2018).

Example-specific Interpretations This section will introduce example-specific interpretations in more detail. We will discuss the challenges and approaches to evaluating such interpretations. We will also cover the critiques and shortcomings of using attention as explanations (Jain and Wallace, 2019; Serrano and Smith, 2019). We will then explain why we focus on *gradient-based methods*: they are model-agnostic, easy to compute, and (largely) faithful to a model's behavior.

Understanding What Parts of An *Input* Led to a Prediction This section will discuss:

- *Saliency maps*, i.e., generating visualizations of "salient" input tokens. We will discuss how to generate saliency maps using gradient-based techniques (Simonyan et al., 2014; Sundararajan et al., 2017; Smilkov et al., 2017)) and black-box techniques (Ribeiro et al., 2016).
- *Input Perturbations*, i.e., showing how changes to the input do (or do not) change the prediction. For example, leave-one-out (Li et al., 2016) and input reduction (Feng et al., 2018). We will also cover *adversarial* perturbations such as token flipping (Ebrahimi et al., 2018) and adding distractor sentences (Jia and Liang, 2017).

Break

Understanding How *Global* Decision Rules Led to a Prediction This section will discuss how certain global "decision rules" can explain model predictions. We will cover Anchors (Ribeiro et al., 2018a) and Universal Adversarial Triggers (Wallace et al., 2019a). We will also discuss how spurious patterns in datasets, e.g., lexical overlap in textual entailment (McCoy et al., 2019), can cause models to learn certain undesirable decision rules.

Understanding Which *Training Examples* Caused a Prediction This section will discuss how to trace model predictions back to the training data, i.e., identifying "influential" training points. We will cover influence functions (Koh and Liang, 2017) and representor points (Yeh et al., 2018).

Coding Interpretations This section will walk through source code for selected interpretation methods. Using AllenNLP Interpret (Wallace et al., 2019b), we will cover example use cases such as interpreting LSTM-based sentiment analysis models and BERT-based masked language models.

Open Problems We will conclude with a discussion of areas for future research:

- *Evaluation:* There is fundamentally no ground-truth to use for evaluating interpretations; how do we define evaluation?
- *Robustness & Faithfulness:* Interpretations may be unfaithful to the underlying model and can be adversarially manipulated. What are the implications of this, and how can we improve existing interpretation methods?
- *Interpretation Beyond Classification:* Most interpretations focus on classification models; how are interpretations best applied to the complex input-output formats seen in NLP tasks (e.g., machine translation)?
- *Closing the loop with Humans:* Humans are the end-users of interpretations; how can we make interpretations interactive, collaborative, customizable, and ultimately more effective?
- *Pretrained Transformer Models:* How do our methods, and the field of interpretability, change with the rise of massively-pretrained models?

4 Instructors

Eric Wallace is a PhD student at the University of California, Berkeley. His research focuses on the interpretability and robustness of machine learning models for NLP. He is the lead developer of the AllenNLP Interpret toolkit and has published numerous papers on interpreting neural NLP models. Website: http://ericswallace.com

Matt Gardner is a senior research scientist at the Allen Institute for Artificial Intelligence (AI2). His research focuses on question answering, semantic parsing, and model analysis. Matt received his PhD from the Language Technologies Institute at Carnegie Mellon University. He is the lead designer of the AllenNLP toolkit and a host of the NLP Highlights podcast.

Matt was an instructor at the Neural Semantic Parsing Tutorial (Gardner et al., 2018a) at ACL 2018, and the Writing Code for NLP Research Tutorial (Gardner et al., 2018c) at EMNLP 2018. Website: https://matt-gardner.github.io/

Sameer Singh is an Assistant Professor of Computer Science at the University of California, Irvine. He is working on large-scale and interpretable machine learning models for NLP. Before UCI, Sameer was a Postdoctoral Research Associate at the University of Washington, and he received his PhD from the University of Massachusetts, Amherst in 2014.

Sameer presented the Deep Adversarial Learning Tutorial (Wang et al., 2019) at NAACL 2019 and the Mining Knowledge Graphs from Text Tutorial at WSDM 2018 and AAAI 2017. Sameer has also received teaching awards at UCI. Website: http://sameersingh.org/

References

Tom B Brown, Benjamin Mann, Nick Ryder, Melanie Subbiah, Jared Kaplan, Prafulla Dhariwal, Arvind Neelakantan, Pranav Shyam, Girish Sastry, Amanda Askell, et al. 2020. Language models are few-shot learners. *arXiv preprint arXiv:2005.14165*.

Jacob Devlin, Ming-Wei Chang, Kenton Lee, and Kristina Toutanova. 2019. BERT: pre-training of deep bidirectional transformers for language understanding. In *NAACL*.

Finale Doshi-Velez and Been Kim. 2017. Towards a rigorous science of interpretable machine learning. *arXiv preprint arXiv:1702.08608*.

Javid Ebrahimi, Daniel Lowd, and Dejing Dou. 2018. On adversarial examples for character-level neural machine translation. In *COLING*.

Shi Feng, Eric Wallace, Alvin Grissom II, Mohit Iyyer, Pedro Rodriguez, and Jordan Boyd-Graber. 2018. Pathologies of neural models make interpretations difficult. In *EMNLP*.

Matt Gardner, Yoav Artzi, Victoria Basmova, Jonathan Berant, Ben Bogin, Sihao Chen, Pradeep Dasigi, Dheeru Dua, Yanai Elazar, Ananth Gottumukkala, et al. 2020. Evaluating NLP models via contrast sets. *arXiv preprint arXiv:2004.02709*.

Matt Gardner, Pradeep Dasigi, Srinivasan Iyer, Alane Suhr, and Luke Zettlemoyer. 2018a. Neural semantic parsing. In *ACL Tutorial*.

Matt Gardner, Joel Grus, Mark Neumann, Oyvind Tafjord, Pradeep Dasigi, Nelson Liu, Matthew Peters, Michael Schmitz, and Luke Zettlemoyer. 2018b. Allennlp: A deep semantic natural language processing platform. In *ACL Workshop for NLP Open Source Software*.

Matt Gardner, Mark Neumann, Joel Grus, and Nicholas Lourie. 2018c. Writing code for NLP research. In *EMNLP*.

Suchin Gururangan, Swabha Swayamdipta, Omer Levy, Roy Schwartz, Samuel R. Bowman, and Noah A. Smith. 2018. Annotation artifacts in natural language inference data. In *NAACL*.

Sarthak Jain and Byron C Wallace. 2019. Attention is not explanation. In *NAACL*.

Robin Jia and Percy Liang. 2017. Adversarial examples for evaluating reading comprehension systems. In *EMNLP*.

Pang Wei Koh and Percy Liang. 2017. Understanding black-box predictions via influence functions. In *ICML*.

Jiwei Li, Will Monroe, and Dan Jurafsky. 2016. Understanding neural networks through representation erasure. *arXiv preprint arXiv:1612.08220*.

Zachary C Lipton. 2018. The mythos of model interpretability. *Queue*.

Nelson F Liu, Matt Gardner, Yonatan Belinkov, Matthew Peters, and Noah A Smith. 2019. Linguistic knowledge and transferability of contextual representations. In *NAACL*.

R Thomas McCoy, Ellie Pavlick, and Tal Linzen. 2019. Right for the wrong reasons: Diagnosing syntactic heuristics in natural language inference. In *ACL*.

Sewon Min, Eric Wallace, Sameer Singh, Matt Gardner, Hannaneh Hajishirzi, and Luke Zettlemoyer. 2019. Compositional questions do not necessitate multi-hop reasoning.

Aakanksha Naik, Abhilasha Ravichander, Norman Sadeh, Carolyn Rose, and Graham Neubig. 2018. Stress test evaluation for natural language inference. In *COLING*.

Matthew E. Peters, Mark Neumann, Mohit Iyyer, Matt Gardner, Christopher Clark, Kenton Lee, and Luke Zettlemoyer. 2018. Deep contextualized word representations. In *NAACL*.

Alec Radford, Jeffrey Wu, Rewon Child, David Luan, Dario Amodei, and Ilya Sutskever. 2019. Language models are unsupervised multitask learners. *Technical report*.

Marco Tulio Ribeiro, Sameer Singh, and Carlos Guestrin. 2016. Why should I trust you?: Explaining the predictions of any classifier. In *KDD*.

Marco Túlio Ribeiro, Sameer Singh, and Carlos Guestrin. 2018a. Anchors: High-precision model-agnostic explanations. In *AAAI*.

Marco Tulio Ribeiro, Sameer Singh, and Carlos Guestrin. 2018b. Semantically equivalent adversarial rules for debugging NLP models. In *ACL*.

Maarten Sap, Dallas Card, Saadia Gabriel, Yejin Choi, and Noah A Smith. 2019. The risk of racial bias in hate speech detection. In *ACL*.

Sofia Serrano and Noah A Smith. 2019. Is attention interpretable? In *ACL*.

Karen Simonyan, Andrea Vedaldi, and Andrew Zisserman. 2014. Deep inside convolutional networks: Visualising image classification models and saliency maps. In *ICLR Workshop*.

Daniel Smilkov, Nikhil Thorat, Been Kim, Fernanda B. Viégas, and Martin Wattenberg. 2017. SmoothGrad: removing noise by adding noise. In *ICML Workshop on Visualization for Deep Learning*.

Mukund Sundararajan, Ankur Taly, and Qiqi Yan. 2017. Axiomatic attribution for deep networks. In *ICML*.

Christian Szegedy, Wojciech Zaremba, Ilya Sutskever, Joan Bruna, Dumitru Erhan, Ian J. Goodfellow, and Rob Fergus. 2014. Intriguing properties of neural networks. In *ICLR*.

Ian Tenney, Patrick Xia, Berlin Chen, Alex Wang, Adam Poliak, R Thomas McCoy, Najoung Kim, Benjamin Van Durme, Samuel R Bowman, Dipanjan Das, and Ellie Pavlick. 2019. What do you learn from context? probing for sentence structure in contextualized word representations. In *ICLR*.

Eric Wallace, Shi Feng, Nikhil Kandpal, Matt Gardner, and Sameer Singh. 2019a. Universal adversarial triggers for attacking and analyzing NLP. In *EMNLP*.

Eric Wallace, Jens Tuyls, Junlin Wang, Sanjay Subramanian, Matt Gardner, and Sameer Singh. 2019b. AllenNLP Interpret: A framework for explaining predictions of NLP models. In *EMNLP*.

William Yang Wang, Sameer Singh, and Jiwei Li. 2019. Deep adversarial learning for NLP. In *NAACL Tutorial*.

Tongshuang Wu, Marco Tulio Ribeiro, Jeffrey Heer, and Daniel S. Weld. 2019. Errudite: Scalable, reproducible, and testable error analysis. In *ACL*.

Chih-Kuan Yeh, Joon Kim, Ian En-Hsu Yen, and Pradeep K Ravikumar. 2018. Representer point selection for explaining deep neural networks. In *NeurIPS*.

High Performance Natural Language Processing

Gabriel Ilharco[†] **Cesar Ilharco**[‡] **Iulia Turc**[‡]
Tim Dettmers[†] **Felipe Ferreira**[‡] **Kenton Lee**[‡]
[†]Paul G. Allen School of Computer Science & Engineering, University of Washington
[‡]Google Research
{gamaga,dettmers}@cs.washington.edu
{ilharco,iuliaturc,felipeg,kentonl}@google.com

Abstract

Scale has played a central role in the rapid progress natural language processing has enjoyed in recent years. While benchmarks are dominated by ever larger models, efficient hardware use is critical for their widespread adoption and further progress in the field. In this cutting-edge tutorial, we will recapitulate the state-of-the-art in natural language processing with scale in perspective. After establishing these foundations, we will cover a wide range of techniques for improving efficiency, including knowledge distillation, quantization, pruning, more efficient architectures, along with case studies and practical implementation tricks.

1 Tutorial Proposal

Recent advances in natural language processing (Radford et al. (2018); Devlin et al. (2018); Liu et al. (2019); Brown et al. (2020), among many others) have substantially improved model capabilities. Notably, pre-trained checkpoints can be fine-tuned without substantial task specific modifications to create powerful models for a wide range of tasks (Wang et al., 2018, 2019). For many applications, production systems with models up to date with the state-of-the-art are meeting high quality bars for adoption across a wide variety of language tasks.

However, the ever larger computational requirements of such cutting-edge models—which quickly approximates the scale of a trillion parameters (Lepikhin et al., 2020)—imposes challenges to their widespread adoption and further progress in the field. This has driven increasing attention to methods that allow more efficient use of hardware, through techniques such as knowledge distillation (Hinton et al., 2015; Turc et al., 2019), quantization (Shen et al., 2020; Zafrir et al., 2019), pruning (Sanh et al., 2020), and architectural changes (Kitaev et al. (2020); Wang et al. (2020b); Katharopoulos et al. (2020); Zaheer et al. (2020), among others). Altogether, these techniques are promising avenues for more efficient natural language processing.

This tutorial starts with an introduction covering recent trends in NLP with scale in perspective, and covers foundational knowledge such as the transformer architecture (Vaswani et al., 2017) and the fine-tuning paradigm. We then move to core techniques for improving efficiency, including knowledge distillation, quantization and pruning, later covering recent work on architectural improvements, focusing on the move towards self-attention with linear complexity. Then, we dive into case studies by examining specific models such as Iandola et al. (2020) and Sun et al. (2020). Finally, we end with practical implementation considerations including model and data parallelism, gradient accumulation and floating point precision, ending the tutorial with closing notes and a questions and answers section. We outline the structure of this tutorial in Table 1.

1.1 Type of the tutorial

Cutting edge.

1.2 Reading list

Fundamentals: Bahdanau et al. (2014); Vaswani et al. (2017); Devlin et al. (2018); Brown et al. (2020); Lepikhin et al. (2020); Nakkiran et al. (2019).

Core techniques: Hinton et al. (2015); Turc et al. (2019); Jiao et al. (2019); Shen et al. (2020); Zafrir et al. (2019); Frankle and Carbin (2018); Brix et al. (2020); Sanh et al. (2020).

Efficient attention: Beltagy et al. (2020); Kitaev et al. (2020); Wang et al. (2020b); Stickland

Proceedings of the 2020 Conference on Empirical Methods in Natural Language Processing: Tutorial Abstracts, pages 24–27
Online, November 19 - 20, 2020.
https://doi.org/10.18653/v1/P17

Section	Subsection	Duration
Introduction	Overview of the field with scale into perspective	10 min
Fundamentals	Self-attention and the transformer architecture	25 min
Core techniques	Knowledge distillation	15 min
	Quantization	15 min
	Pruning	15 min
Efficient attention	Towards linear complexity in attention	30 min
Case studies	Efficient language models	20 min
	Retrieval	10 min
Scaling in practice	Practical considerations for scaling NLP models	35 min
Final considerations	Closing notes, Q&A	5 min
Total	-	180 min

Table 1: Structure of the tutorial with duration of each section.

and Murray (2019); Correia et al. (2019); Vyas et al. (2020); Katharopoulos et al. (2020); Zaheer et al. (2020).

Case studies: Botha et al. (2017); So et al. (2019); Sun et al. (2020); Yan et al. (2020); Wang et al. (2020a); Iandola et al. (2020); Mehta et al. (2020); Reimers and Gurevych (2019); Khandelwal et al. (2019); Guu et al. (2020).

Scaling in practice : Micikevicius et al. (2017); Krizhevsky (2014); Sohoni et al. (2019); Kaplan et al. (2020); Lepikhin et al. (2020)

1.3 Authors

Gabriel Ilharco is a PhD candidate at the University of Washington, where he is advised by Ali Farhadi and Hannaneh Hajishirzi. Previously, he worked at Google Research. His research interests lie at the intersection of Natural Language Processing and Computer Vision. His previous experience in teaching includes the tutorial *Deep Learning for Natural Language Processing with Tensorflow*, at KDD 2019. `http://gabrielilharco.com/`

Cesar Ilharco is a Research Engineer at Google, developing ML models for News Intelligence & Realtime Event Understanding, where performance is important for efficient serving at large scale. He was a guest lecturer and industry partner at Harvard University (ML for knowledge reconciliation), and co-organized the tutorials *Deep Learning for Natural Language Processing with Tensorflow* (KDD 2019) and *Neural Structured Learning: Training neural networks with structured signals* (KDD 2020).

Iulia Turc is a Software Engineer at Google Research, currently working on transfer learning. Her past experience at Google includes federated learning and applied machine learning for various products. Previously, Iulia completed her master's degree at the University of Oxford where she focused on machine translation. `http://www.iuliaturc.com`.

Tim Dettmers is a PhD student at the University of Washington where he is advised by Luke Zettlemoyer. He also works as a visiting researcher at Facebook AI Research, Seattle. His main research interests are large scale NLP models and efficient deep learning. `https://timdettmers.com/about`

Felipe Tiengo Ferreira is a Senior Staff Software Engineer leading News Intelligence and Realtime Event Understanding, an applied research team across Mountain View, NYC, Paris, Vienna and Zurich. Felipe has an expertise in making complex systems—including NLP components—work in real-time at massive scale across different product areas at Google. `https://research.google/people/FelipeGoldstein/`

Kenton Lee is a Research Scientist at Google. His research spans several areas in NLP, including structured prediction, question answering, and transfer learning. Before joining Google Research, Kenton completed a PhD at the University of Washington while working with Luke Zettlemoyer. `https://kentonl.com`.

1.4 Prerequisites

- Math: Basic understanding of probability theory and linear algebra;
- Machine Learning: Basic familiarity with embeddings and sequence-to-sequence models. Familiarity with self-attention, transformers, and large-scale pretraining is desirable;

References

Dzmitry Bahdanau, Kyunghyun Cho, and Yoshua Bengio. 2014. Neural machine translation by jointly learning to align and translate. *arXiv preprint arXiv:1409.0473*.

Iz Beltagy, Matthew E Peters, and Arman Cohan. 2020. Longformer: The long-document transformer. *arXiv preprint arXiv:2004.05150*.

Jan A. Botha, Emily Pitler, Ji Ma, Anton Bakalov, Alex Salcianu, David Weiss, Ryan McDonald, and Slav Petrov. 2017. Natural language processing with small feed-forward networks. *Proceedings of the 2017 Conference on Empirical Methods in Natural Language Processing*.

Christopher Brix, Parnia Bahar, and Hermann Ney. 2020. Successfully applying the stabilized lottery ticket hypothesis to the transformer architecture. *arXiv preprint arXiv:2005.03454*.

Tom B Brown, Benjamin Mann, Nick Ryder, Melanie Subbiah, Jared Kaplan, Prafulla Dhariwal, Arvind Neelakantan, Pranav Shyam, Girish Sastry, Amanda Askell, et al. 2020. Language models are few-shot learners. *arXiv preprint arXiv:2005.14165*.

Gonçalo M. Correia, Vlad Niculae, and André F. T. Martins. 2019. Adaptively sparse transformers. *Proceedings of the 2019 Conference on Empirical Methods in Natural Language Processing and the 9th International Joint Conference on Natural Language Processing (EMNLP-IJCNLP)*.

Jacob Devlin, Ming-Wei Chang, Kenton Lee, and Kristina Toutanova. 2018. Bert: Pre-training of deep bidirectional transformers for language understanding. *arXiv preprint arXiv:1810.04805*.

Jonathan Frankle and Michael Carbin. 2018. The lottery ticket hypothesis: Finding sparse, trainable neural networks.

Kelvin Guu, Kenton Lee, Zora Tung, Panupong Pasupat, and Ming-Wei Chang. 2020. Realm: Retrieval-augmented language model pre-training.

Geoffrey Hinton, Oriol Vinyals, and Jeff Dean. 2015. Distilling the knowledge in a neural network. *arXiv preprint arXiv:1503.02531*.

Forrest N Iandola, Albert E Shaw, Ravi Krishna, and Kurt W Keutzer. 2020. Squeezebert: What can computer vision teach nlp about efficient neural networks? *arXiv preprint arXiv:2006.11316*.

Xiaoqi Jiao, Yichun Yin, Lifeng Shang, Xin Jiang, Xiao Chen, Linlin Li, Fang Wang, and Qun Liu. 2019. Tinybert: Distilling bert for natural language understanding.

Jared Kaplan, Sam McCandlish, Tom Henighan, Tom B Brown, Benjamin Chess, Rewon Child, Scott Gray, Alec Radford, Jeffrey Wu, and Dario Amodei. 2020. Scaling laws for neural language models. *arXiv preprint arXiv:2001.08361*.

Angelos Katharopoulos, Apoorv Vyas, Nikolaos Pappas, and François Fleuret. 2020. Transformers are rnns: Fast autoregressive transformers with linear attention. *arXiv preprint arXiv:2006.16236*.

Urvashi Khandelwal, Omer Levy, Dan Jurafsky, Luke Zettlemoyer, and Mike Lewis. 2019. Generalization through memorization: Nearest neighbor language models.

Nikita Kitaev, Łukasz Kaiser, and Anselm Levskaya. 2020. Reformer: The efficient transformer. *arXiv preprint arXiv:2001.04451*.

Alex Krizhevsky. 2014. One weird trick for parallelizing convolutional neural networks. *arXiv preprint arXiv:1404.5997*.

Dmitry Lepikhin, HyoukJoong Lee, Yuanzhong Xu, Dehao Chen, Orhan Firat, Yanping Huang, Maxim Krikun, Noam Shazeer, and Zhifeng Chen. 2020. Gshard: Scaling giant models with conditional computation and automatic sharding. *arXiv preprint arXiv:2006.16668*.

Yinhan Liu, Myle Ott, Naman Goyal, Jingfei Du, Mandar Joshi, Danqi Chen, Omer Levy, Mike Lewis, Luke Zettlemoyer, and Veselin Stoyanov. 2019. Roberta: A robustly optimized BERT pretraining approach. *CoRR*, abs/1907.11692.

Sachin Mehta, Marjan Ghazvininejad, Srinivasan Iyer, Luke Zettlemoyer, and Hannaneh Hajishirzi. 2020. Delight: Very deep and light-weight transformer. *arXiv preprint arXiv:2008.00623*.

Paulius Micikevicius, Sharan Narang, Jonah Alben, Gregory Diamos, Erich Elsen, David Garcia, Boris Ginsburg, Michael Houston, Oleksii Kuchaiev, Ganesh Venkatesh, et al. 2017. Mixed precision training. *arXiv preprint arXiv:1710.03740*.

Preetum Nakkiran, Gal Kaplun, Yamini Bansal, Tristan Yang, Boaz Barak, and Ilya Sutskever. 2019. Deep double descent: Where bigger models and more data hurt. *arXiv preprint arXiv:1912.02292*.

Alec Radford, Jeffrey Wu, Rewon Child, David Luan, Dario Amodei, and Ilya Sutskever. 2018. Language models are unsupervised multitask learners.

Nils Reimers and Iryna Gurevych. 2019. Sentence-bert: Sentence embeddings using siamese bert-networks. *Proceedings of the 2019 Conference on Empirical Methods in Natural Language Processing and the 9th International Joint Conference on Natural Language Processing (EMNLP-IJCNLP).*

Victor Sanh, Thomas Wolf, and Alexander M Rush. 2020. Movement pruning: Adaptive sparsity by fine-tuning. *arXiv preprint arXiv:2005.07683.*

Sheng Shen, Zhen Dong, Jiayu Ye, Linjian Ma, Zhewei Yao, Amir Gholami, Michael W Mahoney, and Kurt Keutzer. 2020. Q-bert: Hessian based ultra low precision quantization of bert. In *AAAI*, pages 8815–8821.

David R So, Chen Liang, and Quoc V Le. 2019. The evolved transformer. *arXiv preprint arXiv:1901.11117.*

Nimit Sharad Sohoni, Christopher Richard Aberger, Megan Leszczynski, Jian Zhang, and Christopher Ré. 2019. Low-memory neural network training: A technical report. *arXiv preprint arXiv:1904.10631.*

Asa Cooper Stickland and Iain Murray. 2019. Bert and pals: Projected attention layers for efficient adaptation in multi-task learning.

Zhiqing Sun, Hongkun Yu, Xiaodan Song, Renjie Liu, Yiming Yang, and Denny Zhou. 2020. Mobilebert: a compact task-agnostic bert for resource-limited devices. *arXiv preprint arXiv:2004.02984.*

Iulia Turc, Ming-Wei Chang, Kenton Lee, and Kristina Toutanova. 2019. Well-read students learn better: The impact of student initialization on knowledge distillation. *arXiv preprint arXiv:1908.08962.*

Ashish Vaswani, Noam Shazeer, Niki Parmar, Jakob Uszkoreit, Llion Jones, Aidan N Gomez, Łukasz Kaiser, and Illia Polosukhin. 2017. Attention is all you need. In *Advances in neural information processing systems*, pages 5998–6008.

Apoorv Vyas, Angelos Katharopoulos, and François Fleuret. 2020. Fast transformers with clustered attention.

Alex Wang, Yada Pruksachatkun, Nikita Nangia, Amanpreet Singh, Julian Michael, Felix Hill, Omer Levy, and Samuel Bowman. 2019. Superglue: A stickier benchmark for general-purpose language understanding systems. In *Advances in Neural Information Processing Systems*, pages 3266–3280.

Alex Wang, Amanpreet Singh, Julian Michael, Felix Hill, Omer Levy, and Samuel R Bowman. 2018. Glue: A multi-task benchmark and analysis platform for natural language understanding. *arXiv preprint arXiv:1804.07461.*

Hanrui Wang, Zhanghao Wu, Zhijian Liu, Han Cai, Ligeng Zhu, Chuang Gan, and Song Han. 2020a. Hat: Hardware-aware transformers for efficient natural language processing. *Proceedings of the 58th Annual Meeting of the Association for Computational Linguistics.*

Sinong Wang, Belinda Li, Madian Khabsa, Han Fang, and Hao Ma. 2020b. Linformer: Self-attention with linear complexity. *arXiv preprint arXiv:2006.04768.*

Zhongxia Yan, Hanrui Wang, Demi Guo, and Song Han. 2020. Micronet for efficient language modeling. *arXiv preprint arXiv:2005.07877.*

Ofir Zafrir, Guy Boudoukh, Peter Izsak, and Moshe Wasserblat. 2019. Q8bert: Quantized 8bit bert. *arXiv preprint arXiv:1910.06188.*

Manzil Zaheer, Guru Guruganesh, Avinava Dubey, Joshua Ainslie, Chris Alberti, Santiago Ontanon, Philip Pham, Anirudh Ravula, Qifan Wang, Li Yang, et al. 2020. Big bird: Transformers for longer sequences. *arXiv preprint arXiv:2007.14062.*

Representation, Learning and Reasoning on Spatial Language for Downstream NLP Tasks

Parisa Kordjamshidi
Michigan State University
kordjams@msu.edu

James Pustejovsky
Brandeis University
jamesp@cs.brandeis.edu

Marie-Francine Moens
KU Leuven
sien.moens@cs.kuleuven.be

1 Description

This tutorial provides an overview over the *cutting edge* research on *spatial language understanding*. However, we cover some background material from various perspectives given that ACL community has not paid enough attention, in the last two decades, to this topic. There are a few emerging research work very recently looking back into the importance of spatial language in various NLP tasks. One of the essential functions of natural language is to express spatial relationships between objects. Linguistic constructs can encode highly complex, relational structures of objects, spatial relations between them, and patterns of motion through space relative to some reference point. Spatial language understanding is useful in many research areas and real-world applications. This topic recently has attracted the attention of various sub-communities in the intersection of Natural Language, Computer Vision and Robotics. The complexity of spatial language understanding and its importance in downstream tasks that involve grounding the language in the physical world has become to some extent evident to the NLP research community. Compared to other semantically specialized linguistic tasks, standardizing tasks related to spatial language seems to be more challenging as it is harder to obtain an agreeable set of concepts and relationships together with a formal spatial meaning representation that is domain independent (Pustejovsky et al., 2011; Kordjamshidi et al., 2010; Mani, 2009; Pustejovsky, 2017; Dan et al., 2020). For example, compare this with recent work on temporal relations within Computational Linguistics. This has made research results on spatial language learning and reasoning diverse, task-specific and, to some extent, not comparable. While formal meaning representation is a general issue for language understanding, formalizing spatial concepts and building formal reasoning and machine learning models based on those constitute challenging research problems with a wealth of prior foundational work that can be exploited and linked to language understanding.

In this tutorial, we overview four themes: **1) Spatial Semantic Representation; 2) Spatial Information Extraction and; 3) Spatial qualitative representation and reasoning 4) Downstream applications of spatial semantic extraction and spatial reasoning including language grounding, robotics, navigation, dialogue systems and tasks that require combining vision and language.**

The semantic representation section covers the works that have attempted to arrive at a common set of basic concepts and relationships (Bateman, 2010; Hois and Kutz, 2011), as well as making existing corpora interoperable (Pustejovsky et al., 2011; Mani and Pustejovsky, 2012; Kordjamshidi et al., 2017; Kordjamshidi, 2013). We discuss the existing qualitative and quantitative representation and reasoning models that can be used for investigation of interoperabiltiy of machine learning and reasoning over spatial semantics (Cohn et al., 1997). Spatial language meaning representation includes research related to cognitive and linguistically motivated spatial semantic representations, spatial knowledge representation and spatial ontologies, qualitative and quantitative representation models used for formal meaning representation, and various spatial annotation schema and efforts for creating specialized corpora. We discuss various datasets that either focus on spatial annotations or downstream tasks that need spatial language learning and reasoning. Particularly, natural language visual reasoning data (Suhr et al., 2017, 2018). Moreover, continuous meaning representations for spatial concepts is another aspect to be highlighted in the tutorial, e.g., (Collell Talleda and Moens, 2018; Collell Talleda et al., 2018; Deruyt-

Proceedings of the 2020 Conference on Empirical Methods in Natural Language Processing: Tutorial Abstracts, pages 28–33
Online, November 19 - 20, 2020.
https://doi.org/10.18653/v1/P17

tere et al.).

We overview the state-of-the-art for extraction of spatial information from language, both the abstract semantic extraction (Kordjamshidi et al., 2011; Kordjamshidi and Moens, 2015) and extraction that is driven by various target tasks and applications. We discuss machine learning models including structured output prediction models, deep learning architectures and probabilistic graphical models that have been used in the related work.

Finally, we overview the usage of spatial semantics by various downstream tasks and killer applications including language grounding, navigation, self-driving cars, robotics (Tellex et al., 2011; Kollar et al., 2010), dialogue systems (Kelleher and Kruijff, 2006) and human machine interaction, and geographical information systems and knowledge graphs (Stock et al., 2013; Mai et al., 2020). Spatial semantics is very closely connected and relevant to visualization of natural language and grounding language into perception, central to dealing with configurations in the physical world and motivating a combination of vision and language for richer spatial understanding. The related tasks include: text-to-scene conversion; image captioning; spatial and visual question answering; and spatial understanding in multimodal settings (Rahgooy et al., 2018) for robotics and navigation tasks and language grounding (Thomason et al., 2018).

The current research using end-to-end monolithic deep models fail to solve complex tasks that need deep language understanding and reasoning capabilities (Hudson and Manning, 2019). Throughout this proposal, we will highlight the importance of combining learning and reasoning for spatial language understanding and its influence on the semantic representation and type of the learning models as well as the performance on various applications. Regarding the question of reasoning, we (a) point out the role of qualitative and quantitative formal representations in helping spatial reasoning based on natural language and the possibility of learning such representations from data to support compositionality and inference (Hudson and Manning, 2018; Hu et al., 2017); and (b) examine how continuous representations contribute to supporting reasoning and alternative hypothesis formation in learning (Krishnaswamy et al., 2019). We point to the cutting edge research that shows the influence of explicit representation of spatial entities and concepts (Hu et al., 2019; Liu et al., 2019). The main goal of this tutorial is to combine these current related efforts from different communities and application domains into one unified treatment, to identify the challenges, problems and future directions for spatial language understanding.

2 Outline

The tutorial will cover the following syllabus:

- Spatial Representations
  - Linguistic corpora and semantic annotations
  - Spatial knowledge representation and spatial calculi models
  - Distributed representations
- Spatial Information Extraction
  - Spatial entity and relation extraction
  - Spatial ontology population
  - Considering domain knowledge and pragmatics in spatial extractions
- Spatial Semantic Grounding
  - Combining vision and language (symbolic and multimodal embeddings)
  - Capturing spatial common sense
  - Grounding language in 2D and 3D physical worlds
  - Generating referring expressions
- Spatial Reasoning
  - Overview on natural language and visual reasoning tasks and data
  - Modeling compositionality and spatial reasoning in (Deep) learning models
- Downstream tasks
  - Spatial concepts in dialogue systems
  - Spatial reasoning for QA and VQA
  - HRI, navigation and way-finding instructions
  - Corpus-based GIS systems

3 Prerequisites and reading list

Familiarity with machine learning and natural language processing will be helpful for this tutorial. Our selected reading list is as follows.

- Qualitative spatial representation and reasoning. Anthony G. Cohn, and Jochen Renz. Foundations of Artificial Intelligence 3 (2008): 551-596. `http://dai.fmph.uniba.sk/~sefranek/kri/handbook/chapter13.pdf`

- A linguistic ontology of space for natural language processing. John A. Bateman, Joana Hois, Robert Ross, and Thora Tenbrink. Artificial Intelligence 174, no. 14 (2010): 1027-1071. `https://core.ac.uk/download/pdf/82158176.pdf`

- Spatial Role Labeling: Task Definition and Annotation Scheme. Parisa Kordjamshidi, Marie-Francine Moens, Martijn van Otterlo, (2010). Proceedings of the Seventh conference on International Language Resources and Evaluation (LREC'10).

- The qualitative spatial dynamics of motion in language. James Pustejovsky, and Jessica L. Moszkowicz. Spatial Cognition Computation 11, no. 1 (2011): 15-44. `http://www.cs-135.org/wp-content/uploads/2017/12/SCC-2011.pdf`

- Interpreting Motion: Grounded Representations for Spatial Language. Inderjeet Mani and James Pustejovsky (2012), Explorations in language and space. Oxford University Press.

- Changing perspective: Local alignment of reference frames in dialogue, Simon Dobnik, Christine Howes, JD Kelleher, Proceedings of SEMDIAL (goDIAL), 24-32, 2015.

- Global machine learning for spatial ontology population. Parisa Kordjamshidi, Marie-Francine Moens, (2015). Journal of Web Semantics, 30, 3-21.

- VoxML: A Visualization Modeling Language. James Pustejovsky, and Nikhil Krishnaswamy. In Proceedings of the Tenth International Conference on Language Resources and Evaluation (LREC'16), pp. 4606-4613. 2016. `https://arxiv.org/pdf/1610.01508.pdf`

- Do you see what I see? effects of pov on spatial relation specifications. Nikhil Krishnaswamy, and James Pustejovsky. In Proc. 30th International Workshop on Qualitative Reasoning. 2017. `http://qrg.northwestern.edu/qr2017/papers/QR2017_paper_4.pdf`

- ISO-Space: Annotating static and dynamic spatial information. James Pustejovsky (2017). In Handbook of Linguistic Annotation, pages 989–1024. Springer.

- Spatial role labeling annotation scheme. Parisa Kordjamshidi, Martijn van Otterlo, Marie-Francine Moens, (2017). In: Pustejovsky J., Ide N. (Eds.), Handbook of Linguistic Annotation Springer Verlag.

- Source-target inference models for spatial instruction understanding. Hao Tan and Mohit Bansal (2018). In Proceedings of the Thirty-Second AAAI Conference on Artificial Intelligence (AAAI-18) (5504-5511). `https://arxiv.org/abs/1707.03804`

- Acquiring common sense spatial knowledge through implicit spatial templates. Guillem Collell, Luc Van Gool and Marie-Francine Moens (2018). In Proceedings of the Thirty-Second AAAI Conference on Artificial Intelligence (AAAI 2018) (pp. 6765-6772). AAAI. `https://arxiv.org/abs/1711.06821`

- Generating a Novel Dataset of Multimodal Referring Expressions. Nikhil Krishnaswamy, and James Pustejovsky. In Proceedings of the 13th International Conference on Computational Semantics, pp. 44-51. 2019. `https://www.aclweb.org/anthology/W19-0507.pdf`

4 Instructors

- **Parisa Kordjamshidi** is Assistant Professor of Computer Science Department at Michigan State University. Her research interests are in NLP and Machine learning. She has been working on spatial semantics extraction and annotation schemes, mapping language to formal spatial representations, spatial ontologies, structured output prediction models for information extraction, combining vision and language for spatial language understanding. She has been organizing/co-organizing shared tasks on Spatial role labeling, SpRL-2012, SpRL-2013 and the Space Evaluation workshop, SpaceEval-2015, in SemEval Series and Multimodal spatial role labeling workshop mSpRL at CLEF-2017 with the goal of considering vision and language media for spatial information extraction and organized SpLU-2018 and Robonlp-SpLU collocated with NAACL-18 and NAACL-2019 respectively.

Contact information. Email: kordjams@msu.edu, Phone: +1-2174187004, Address: Engineering Building 428 S. Shaw Lane, East Lansing, MI 48824, USA. Webpage: `http://www.cse.msu.edu/~kordjams`.

- **James Pustejovsky** is the TJX Feldberg Chair in Computer Science at Brandeis University, where he is also Chair of the Linguistics Program, Chair of the Computational Linguistics MA Program, and Director of the Lab for Linguistics and Computation. He received his B.S. from MIT and his Ph.D. from UMASS at Amherst. He has worked on computational and lexical semantics for 25 years and is chief developer of Generative Lexicon Theory. Since 2002, he has been working on the development of a platform for temporal reasoning in language, called TARSQI (www.tarsqi.org). Pustejovsky is chief architect of TimeML and ISO-TimeML, a recently adopted ISO standard for temporal information in language, as well as the recently adopted standard, ISO-Space, a specification for spatial information in language. He has developed a modeling framework for representing linguistic expressions and interactions as multimodal simulations. This platform, VoxML, enables real-time communication between humans and computers or robots for joint tasks, utilizing speech, gesture, gaze, and action. He is currently working with robotics researchers in IHRI to allow the VoxML platform to act as both a dialogue management system as well as a simulation environment that reveals realtime epistemic state and perceptual input to a computational agent. His areas of interest include: Computational semantics, temporal and spatial reasoning, language annotation for machine.

Contact Information. Email: pustejovsky@gmail.com, jamesp@cs.brandeis.edu, Phone: +1-781-736-2709, Address : Dept. of Computer Science, Brandeis University, 415 South Street, MS-018, Waltham, MA 02454, USA. Web-page: `http://www.pusto.com`.

- **Marie-Francine Moens** is Full Professor at the Department of Computer Science, KU Leuven. She has a special interest in machine learning for natural language understanding and in grounding language in a visual context. She is holder of the prestiguous ERC Advanced Grant CALCULUS (2018-2023) granted by the European Research Council on the topic of language understanding. She is currently associate editor of the journal IEEE Transactions on Pattern Analysis and Machine Intelligence (TPAMI). In 2011 and 2012 she was appointed as chair of the European Chapter of the Association for Computational Linguistics (EACL) and was a member of the executive board of the Association for Computational Linguistics (ACL). From 2014 till 2018 she was the scientific manager of the EU COST action iVL Net (The European Network on Integrating Vision and Language).

Contact information. Email: sien.moens@cs.kuleuven.be, Phone: +32 16 32 83 53, Address: Department of Computer Science, KU Leuven, Celestijnenlaan 200A, B-3001 Heverlee, Belgium. Webpage: `https://people.cs.kuleuven.be/~sien.moens`

5 Acknowledgements

This project is supported by National Science Foundation (NSF) CAREER award #1845771.

References

J. A. Bateman. 2010. Language and space: A two-level semantic approach based on principles of ontological engineering. *International Journal of Speech Technology*, 13(1):29–48.

Anthony G. Cohn, Brandon Bennett, John Gooday, and Nicholas M. Gotts. 1997. Representing and reasoning with qualitative spatial relations. In Oliviero Stock, editor, *Spatial and Temporal Reasoning*, pages 97–132. Springer.

Guillem Collell Talleda and Marie-Francine Moens. 2018. Learning representations specialized in spatial knowledge: Leveraging language and vision. *Transactions of the Association for Computational Linguistics*, 6:133–144.

Guillem Collell Talleda, Luc Van Gool, and Marie-Francine Moens. 2018. Acquiring common sense spatial knowledge through implicit spatial templates. In *Proceedings of Thirty-Second AAAI Conference on Artificial Intelligence (AAAI-18)*, pages 6765–6772. AAAI.

Soham Dan, Parisa Kordjamshidi, Julia Bonn, Archna Bhatia, Martha Palmer, and Dan Roth. 2020. In *Proceedings of Language Resources and Evaluation Conference, LREC-2020*.

Thierry Deruyttere, Simon Vandenhende, Dusan Grujicic, Luc Van Gool, and Marie-Francine Moens. Talk2car: Taking control of your self driving car. In *Proceedings of the 2019 Conference on Empirical Methods in Natural Language Processing and 9th International Joint Conference on Natural Language Processing*, EMNLP 2019. ACL.

Johana Hois and Oliver Kutz. 2011. Towards linguistically-grounded spatial logics. In *Spatial Representation and Reasoning in Language: Ontologies and Logics of Space*, number 10131 in Dagstuhl Seminar Proceedings. Schloss Dagstuhl - Leibniz-Zentrum fuer Informatik, Germany.

Ronghang Hu, Jacob Andreas, Marcus Rohrbach, Trevor Darrell, and Kate Saenko. 2017. Learning to reason: End-to-end module networks for visual question answering. *2017 IEEE International Conference on Computer Vision (ICCV)*, pages 804–813.

Ronghang Hu, Daniel Fried, Anna Rohrbach, Dan Klein, Trevor Darrell, and Kate Saenko. 2019. Are you looking? grounding to multiple modalities in vision-and-language navigation. In *Proceedings of the 57th Conference of the Association for Computational Linguistics, ACL 2019, Florence, Italy, July 28- August 2, 2019, Volume 1: Long Papers*, pages 6551–6557.

Drew A Hudson and Christopher D Manning. 2018. Compositional attention networks for machine reasoning. In *International Conference on Learning Representations (ICLR)*.

Drew A Hudson and Christopher D Manning. 2019. GQA: A new dataset for real-world visual reasoning and compositional question answering. *Conference on Computer Vision and Pattern Recognition (CVPR)*.

John D. Kelleher and Geert-Jan M. Kruijff. 2006. Incremental generation of spatial referring expressions in situated dialog. In *Proceedings of the 21st International Conference on Computational Linguistics and 44th Annual Meeting of the Association for Computational Linguistics*, pages 1041–1048, Sydney, Australia. Association for Computational Linguistics.

T. Kollar, S. Tellex, D. Roy, and N. Roy. 2010. Toward understanding natural language directions. In *Proceeding of the 5th ACM/IEEE International Conference on Human-Robot Interaction*, HRI '10, pages 259–266. ACM.

Parisa Kordjamshidi. 2013. *Structured machine learning for mapping natural language to spatial ontologies*. Ph.D. thesis, KULeuven.

Parisa Kordjamshidi and Marie-Francine Moens. 2015. Global machine learning for spatial ontology population. *Web Semant.*, 30(C):3–21.

Parisa Kordjamshidi, Martijn van Otterlo, and Marie-Francine Moens. 2017. Spatial role labeling annotation scheme. In N. Ide James Pustejovsky, editor, *Handbook of Linguistic Annotation*. Springer Verlag.

Parisa Kordjamshidi, Martijn van Otterlo, and Marie-Francine Moens. 2010. Spatial role labeling: task definition and annotation scheme. In *Proceedings of the Seventh Conference on International Language Resources and Evaluation (LREC'10)*, pages 413–420.

Parisa Kordjamshidi, Martijn van Otterlo, and Marie-Francine Moens. 2011. Spatial role labeling: towards extraction of spatial relations from natural language. *ACM - Transactions on Speech and Language Processing*, 8:1–36.

Nikhil Krishnaswamy, Scott Friedman, and James Pustejovsky. 2019. Combining deep learning and qualitative spatial reasoning to learn complex structures from sparse examples with noise. In *Proceedings of the thirty-third AAAI Conference on Artificial Intelligence*.

Yunchao Liu, Jiajun Wu, Zheng Wu, Daniel Ritchie, William T. Freeman, and Joshua B. Tenenbaum. 2019. Learning to describe scenes with programs. In *International Conference on Learning Representations*.

Gengchen Mai, Krzysztof Janowicz, Ling Cai, Rui Zhu, Blake Regalia, Bo Yan, Meilin Shi, and Ni Lao. 2020. Se-kge: A location-aware knowledge graph embedding model for geographic question answering and spatial semantic lifting. *Transactions in GIS*, 24(3):623–655.

I. Mani and James Pustejovsky. 2012. *Interpreting Motion: Grounded Representations for Spatial Language*. Explorations in language and space. Oxford University Press.

Inderjeet Mani. 2009. SpatialML: annotation scheme for marking spatial expression in natural language. Technical Report Version 3.0, The MITRE Corporation.

James Pustejovsky. 2017. Iso-space: Annotating static and dynamic spatial information. In *Handbook of Linguistic Annotation*, pages 989–1024. Springer.

James Pustejovsky, J. Moszkowicz, and M. Verhagen. 2011. ISO-Space: The annotation of spatial information in language. In *ACL-ISO International Workshop on Semantic Annotation (ISA'6)*.

Taher Rahgooy, Umar Manzoor, and Parisa Kordjamshidi. 2018. Visually guided spatial relation extraction from text. In *Proceedings of The 16th*

Annual Conference of the North American Chapter of the Association for Computational Linguistics, NAACL HLT 2018.

Kristin Stock, Robert C. Pasley, Zoe Gardner, Paul Brindley, Jeremy Morley, and Claudia Cialone. 2013. Creating a corpus of geospatial natural language. In *Spatial Information Theory*, pages 279–298, Cham. Springer International Publishing.

Alane Suhr, Mike Lewis, James Yeh, and Yoav Artzi. 2017. A corpus of natural language for visual reasoning. In *ACL.*

Alane Suhr, Stephanie Zhou, Iris Zhang, Huajun Bai, and Yoav Artzi. 2018. A corpus for reasoning about natural language grounded in photographs. *arXiv preprint arXiv:1811.00491.*

S. Tellex, T. Kollar, S. Dickerson, M. R. Walter, A. G. Banerjee, S. Teller, and N. Roy. 2011. Understanding natural language commands for robotic navigation and mobile manipulation. In *Proceedings of the National Conference on Artificial Intelligence (AAAI).*

Jesse Thomason, Jivko Sinapov, Raymond Mooney, and Peter Stone. 2018. Guiding exploratory behaviors for multi-modal grounding of linguistic descriptions. In *Proceedings of the Thirty-Second AAAI Conference on Artificial Intelligence (AAAI-18).*

Simultaneous Translation

Liang Huang [1,2] **Colin Cherry** [3] **Mingbo Ma** [2] **Naveen Arizhabagan** [3] **Zhongjun He** [4]
[1]Oregon State University [2]Baidu Research USA [3]Google, Inc. [4]Baidu, Inc.

1 Brief Description

Simultaneous translation, which performs translation concurrently with the source speech, is widely useful in many scenarios such as international conferences, negotiations, press releases, legal proceedings, and medicine. This problem has long been considered one of the hardest problems in AI and one of its holy grails. Recently, with rapid improvements in machine translation, speech recognition, and speech synthesis, there has been exciting progress towards simultaneous translation. This tutorial will focus on the design and evaluation of policies for simultaneous translation, to leave attendees with a deep technical understanding of the history, the recent advances, and remaining challenges in this field.

2 Type of the Tutorial

This is a **cutting-edge** proposal, and the **first tutorial** on this topic (simultaneous translation) in the history of ACL, EMNLP, NAACL, EACL, COLING, and AACL.

3 Outline

- Background: Simultaneous Interpretation (15 min.)
- Overview of Challenges and Existing Approaches to Simultaneous Translation (25 min.)
  - tradeoff between quality and latency
  - drastic word orders difference
  - robustness, such as error propagation
- Prefix-to-Prefix Framework and Fixed-Latency Policies (15 min.)
- Latency Metrics (20 min.)
  - Average Proportion (AP)
  - Consecutive Wait (CW)
  - Average Lagging (AL)
  - Differentiable Average Lagging (DAL)
  - Ear-to-Voice Span (EVS)
- Dynamic Policies, Part I (15 min.)
  - Adaptive policy with manually designed criteria
  - Reinforcement Learning-based methods
  - Supervised policy-learning framework
- (Coffee Break)
- Dynamic Policies, Part II: Recent Advances (30 min.)
  - Monotonic Infinite Lookback attention
  - Context-Aware translation
- Dataset for Training and Evaluating Simultaneous Translation (20 min.)
  - Rewriting (paraphrasing) references of parallel text
  - Simultaneous Translation datasets:
    - ∗ UN corpus
    - ∗ EPIC corpus
    - ∗ NAIST dataset
    - ∗ BSTC dataset
- Towards Simultaneous Speech-to-Speech Translation (20 min.)
- Practical System and Products (20 min.)
  - Practical Issues (segmentation, punctuation, error tolerance)
  - speech-to-text and speech-to-speech systems
  - computer aided interpretation (CAI)

Proceedings of the 2020 Conference on Empirical Methods in Natural Language Processing: Tutorial Abstracts, pages 34–36
Online, November 19 - 20, 2020.
https://doi.org/10.18653/v1/P17

4 Breadth

We envision a tutorial that emphasizes interdisciplinary breadth at the beginning and end (roughly one half of the tutorial in total). The beginning section on Human Interpretation will allow us to discuss the strategies and behaviours that enable humans to perform this challenging task, touching on observations from Translation Studies. Meanwhile, the end sections on Practical Issues and Moving Toward Speech to Speech Translation will allow us to discuss issues in incremental Speech Recognition and Text-to-Speech that are otherwise under-represented at a typical *ACL conference.

At most 33% are work by the presenters, and at least 77% are work by other researchers.

5 Diversity

Simultaneous translation techniques can greatly improve the efficiency of human communication across linguistic barriers. With this technology, you will be able to understand any foreign language by pulling out your smart phone to listen to the machine-generated simultaneous translation in your own language, with only less than 3 seconds delay. If you travel to a remote country, you will also be able to "talk" to the locals with this technology using your smart phone and headsets.

Both Mingbo Ma and Naveen Arivazhagan are junior instructors. Colin Cherry works at Google in Montreal, Liang Huang works Oregon State University in Corvallis, and Zhongjun He works at Baidu in Beijing.

6 Prerequisites

- Machine Learning: understand the basics of the sequence-to-sequence framework.
- Linguistics: understand basic syntactic structures and appreciate the vast amount of diversity of syntactic structures (esp. word order) among human languages

7 Small Reading List

Only the last two (33%) were co-authored by the presenters.

- Alvin Grissom II, He He, Jordan Boyd-Graber, John Morgan, and Hal Daumé III, Don't Until the Final Verb Wait: Reinforcement Learning for Simultaneous Machine Translation, EMNLP 2014.

  When source and target language have drastically word orders difference, e.g., from verb-final languages (German) to verb-medial languages (English), the final inal verb is predicted in advance on source side to avoid long latency.

- He He, Alvin Grissom II, Jordan Boyd-Graber and Hal Daumé III, Syntax-based Rewriting for Simultaneous Machine Translation, EMNLP 2015.

  A sentence rewriting method is proposed to generates more monotonic translations to improve the speed-accuracy tradeof. Several grammaticality and meaning-preserving syntactic transformation rules are applied to paraphrase reference translations to make their word order closer to the source language word order.

- Kyunghyun Cho and Masha Esipova, Can neural machine translation do simultaneous translation?, arXiv:1606.02012, 2016.

  Several waiting criteria are manually designed to serve as translation polices to decide wait or read.

- Jiatao Gu, Graham Neubig, Kyunghyun Cho and Victor O.K. Li, Learning to Translate in Real-time with Neural Machine Translation, EACL 2017.

  The authors proposed a NMT framework for simultaneous translation with a agent which learn to make decisions on when to translate or wait by interacting with a pre-trained NMT environment.

- Mingbo Ma, Liang Huang, Hao Xiong, Renjie Zheng, Kaibo Liu, Baigong Zheng, Chuanqiang Zhang, Zhongjun He, Hairong Liu, Xing Li, Hua Wu and Haifeng Wang, STACL: Simultaneous Translation with Implicit Anticipation and Controllable Latency using Prefix-to-Prefix Framework, ACL 2019.

  Prefix-to-prefix framework is proposed for simultaneous translation which implicitly learns to anticipate in a single translation model. Within this framework, "wait-k" policy is trained to generate the target sentence simultaneously with the source sentence with k word delay.

- Naveen Arivazhagan, Colin Cherry, Wolfgang Macherey, Chung-Cheng Chiu, Semih Yavuz, Ruoming Pang Wei Li and Colin Raffel, Monotonic Infinite Lookback Attention for Simultaneous Machine Translation, ACL 2019.

  A Monotonic Infinite Lookback (MILk) technique is proposed to maintain both a hard, monotonic attention head to schedule the reading of the source sentence, and a soft attention head to extend from the monotonic head back to the beginning of the source. MILk is trained to learn a adaptive schedule by balancing the latency-quality trade-offs.

8 Presenters

- **Liang Huang** is an Assistant Professor at Oregon State University and a Distinguished Scientist of Baidu Research USA. He received a Best Paper Award at ACL 2008 and a Best Paper Honorable Mention at EMNLP 2016. He is an award-winning teacher and has given four (4) popular tutorials in COLING 2008, NAACL 2009, ACL 2014, and ACL 2015. He gave an invited talk at ACL 2019 on simultaneous translation.

- **Colin Cherry** is a research scientist at Google. He currently serves as secretary of NAACL and an action editor of TACL. He received Best Paper Award at NAACL 2009. He co-organized two workshops on deep learning for low-resource languages: DeepLo 2018 (at ACL 2018) and DeepLo 2019 (at EMNLP 2019). He also served as research program co-chair for AMTA 2018.

- **Mingbo Ma** is a Senior Research Scientist at Baidu Research USA. He received his Ph.D. from Oregon State University. He is a leading expert in simultaneous translation, and has published 4 papers on this topic.

- **Naveen Arizhabagan** is a Software Engineer at Google. He received BS from UIUC and MS from Stanford. He works on simultaneous translation, speech translation, zero-shot translation, and multilingual translation.

- **Zhongjun He** is a Distinguished Architect of Baidu Inc. He leads Baidu machine translation team and has released several versions of Baidu's simultaneous translation system since 2017. He organized the first simultaneous translation evaluation campaign in China in 2019 and released the Baidu Speech Translation Corpus.

9 Estimated Audience Size

150–200.

10 Special Technical Requirements

Internet access

11 Venue Preference

- First Choice: ACL
- Second Choice: EMNLP

12 Open Access

All materials (slides, videos, etc.) will be openly available online.

The Amazing World of Neural Language Generation

Yangfeng Ji [1] **Antoine Bosselut** [2,3] **Thomas Wolf** [4] **Asli Celikyilmaz** [5]
[1] University of Virginia
[2] Allen Institute for Artificial Intelligence, Seattle, WA, USA
[3] Paul G. Allen School of Computer Science & Engineering, Seattle, WA, USA
[4] Huggingface Inc.
[5] Microsoft Research, Redmond, WA, USA
yangfeng@virginia.edu, antoineb@cs.washington.edu
thomwolf@gmail.com, aslicel@microsoft.com

Abstract

Neural Language Generation (NLG) – using neural network models to generate coherent text – is among the most promising methods for automated text creation. Recent years have seen a paradigm shift in neural text generation, caused by the advances in deep contextual language modeling (e.g., LSTMs, GPT, GPT2) and transfer learning (e.g., ELMo, BERT). While these tools have dramatically improved the state of NLG, particularly for low resources tasks, state-of-the-art NLG models still face many challenges: a lack of diversity in generated text, commonsense violations in depicted situations, difficulties in making use of factual information, and difficulties in designing reliable evaluation metrics. In this tutorial, we will present an overview of the current state-of-the-art in neural network architectures, and how they shaped recent research directions in text generation. We will discuss how and why these models succeed/fail at generating coherent text, and provide insights on several applications.

Type. Cutting-edge.

1 Introduction

Natural Language Generation (NLG) forms the basis of many Natural Language Processing (NLP) tasks such as document summarization, machine translation, image captioning, conversational dialogue, and creative writing, making it an essential component in human-machine communication tasks. With recent progress in training deep neural networks, there has been a paradigm shift from template based approaches to neural methods as the predominant building blocks for text generation systems. Specifically, the rich representation learning capabilities of neural networks have allowed NLG models to be trained directly from large amounts of training data, significantly reducing the need for manual feature engineering.

Many benefits have emerged from this new research direction. First, the prototypical framework for training neural networks in an end-to-end fashion has allowed for a diverse array of contextual information to be incorporable into text generation systems (Vaswani et al., 2017; Radford et al., 2019; Ziegler et al., 2019; Keskar et al., 2019), allowing for a richer range of stylistic variability in generated text. Simultaneously, the combination of deep neural networks, large-scale text data and cheap computational power has accelerated new developments in neural network language models.

However, NLG models still raise many challenges which are the focus of a growing body of work. Examples of such limitations are the lack of diversity in generated texts, difficulty in controlling the discourse coherence of the generated text, the lack of commonsense in generated outputs, an uncertain reliance on provided factual information, and more general open questions on architecture design and optimization settings.

In this tutorial, we will start with an introduction to neural language generation, presenting neural language models and encoder-decoder models. We will then discuss the capabilities and limitations of recent text generation models, the suitable architectures for text generation in various specific applications, and then provide insights into why and how these generation models can be adapted for a particular task (Wiseman et al., 2017; Li et al., 2017; See et al., 2017; Xie, 2017). The discussion on evaluation metrics will start from n-gram matching up to the recent progress on text generation evaluation metrics. In the end, this tutorial will be concluded by presenting and discussing major current research directions in the field of neural language generation. All materials (including slides, code, and demos) will be publicly available online on the day of the tutorial. We do not assume any particular prior knowl-

Proceedings of the 2020 Conference on Empirical Methods in Natural Language Processing: Tutorial Abstracts, pages 37–42
Online, November 19 - 20, 2020. ©2020 Association for Computational Linguistics
https://doi.org/10.18653/v1/P17

edge in text generation or language modeling. Familiarity with standard neural network modules (LSTM/CNN/Transformer) is a plus but not required. The intended length of the tutorial is 3 hours, including a coffee break.

2 Tutorial Goal and Description

2.1 Overview

This tutorial will mainly focus on the recent advances in neural networks for language generation and will have minimal coverage on traditional methods. We will provide an overview on the recent progress of neural language generation for those working in this research area, and will also introduce this exciting research area to the NLP researchers who are not familiar with newest advancements in neural text generation. This tutorial is designed for anyone who has basic knowledge background of NLP or deep learning, which makes it accessible to any attendee of an NLP conference.

2.2 Tutorial Organization

Fundamentals and Progression of Neural Text Generation. Interest in neural text generation was recently catalyzed by the renaissance of neural network research in natural language processing, particularly with the development of neural language models and encoder-decoder models. Requiring minimal templates and hand-designed rules, unlike classical language generation methods, neural language generation models massively reduce the time needed to design and build new text generation system.

In particular, language models and encoder-decoder models conveniently allows to incorporate contexts such as previous or parallel sentences, as exemplified in machine translation models. However the spectrum of applications of NLG systems extends far beyond machine translation and can involve: (1) complex reasoning processes that go behind semantically preserving mapping from one language to another, for instance to model discourse, dialog flows or multi-hop reasoning; (2) a wide range of context information, from memory to multi-modalities like images or speech; and (3) challenging evaluation, as multiple generated outputs can be simultaneously valid for a given context (so called high-entropy tasks). The tutorial will highlight some these topics and provide a comprehensive overview of the advances of neural language generation.

Technical Details for Training and Optimization Neural Text Generation. Many of the recent progresses in neural language generation can be characterized as approaches to address some of the above mentioned issues. By investigating the difference between language generation and other sequential modeling problems, novel training methods (e.g., reinforcement learning or imitation learning) can be designed to capture long-term dependencies in generation. New decoding methods like top-k (Fan et al., 2018), nucleus sampling (Holtzman et al., 2019) or penalized sampling (Keskar et al., 2019) are invented to resolve the diversity issues.

Eventually, smarter ways to incorporate various contextual information in neural network models (Golovanov et al., 2019; Ziegler et al., 2019; Radford et al., 2019; Keskar et al., 2019) provide more flexibility as well as a better reliance of the model on the conditioning inputs.

Evaluation of Text Generation. Finally, there is a formidable challenge in getting better metrics to evaluate the quality of generated texts that stems from open-ended nature of these models output. Leveraging recent advances in representation learning, the field of neural language generation has been able to move beyond evaluation methods based on n-gram matching and incorporate promising approaches to design more reliable evaluation metrics. This tutorial will cover recent progress in this field as well as highlighting pressing issues with the current state of experimental reporting in NLG. Together with evaluation, we will overview several text generation benchmarks commonly used in the field.

Lessons Learned, Future Directions and Practical Advances of Neural Text Geneation. The last part of this tutorial will discuss practical issues when using cutting-edge language generation techniques. Most of the content covered in this part will have corresponding code or demo implemented in a standard deep learning framework like PyTorch or TensorFlow. The concluding part of the tutorial, we will provide a summary of current and future research direction as well as of some open questions to open the discussion.

3 Diversity and Inclusion

Diversity. The background of the instructors of this tutorial is evenly distributed among academia and industry. The instructors consist of a group of researchers ranging from an assistant professor at University of Virginia (Yangfeng Ji), a senior Ph.D. student at University of Washington with years of industry research experience (Antoine Bosselut) and two senior research scientists in industry (Thomas Wolf and Asli Celikyilmaz), who both have years of industry research experience. The tutorial instructors are also from different countries and continents (the Netherlands and USA).

4 Outline

4.1 Schedule

The tutorial will be 3 hours long.

1. **Introduction of Natural Language Generation** (15 minutes long): This section will introduce the tutorial by presenting the recent impact of neural network modeling approaches on the field. We will briefly overview the classical text generation pipeline, and introduce basic building blocks of neural text generation: language modeling and the encoder-decoder frameworks. We will also discuss the limitations of the simple encoder-decoder frameworks and motivate the rest of the tutorial.

2. **Building blocks of Neural Network Models for Language Generation** (60 minutes long): This section will comprise three closely related topics corresponding to three fundamental aspects of building a neural language generation system: (1) selecting the architecture of the model among a variety of choices such as pre-trained language models (Devlin et al., 2018; Radford et al., 2019), variational autoencoders (Bowman et al., 2016; Hu et al., 2017), generative adversarial networks (Fedus et al., 2018; Subramanian et al., 2018), or neural template based methods (Wiseman et al., 2018; Xu et al., 2018); (2) training the model using techniques which can range from simple maximum likelihood estimate up to more advanced training techniques like scheduled sampling (Bengio et al., 2015), unlikelihood training (Welleck et al., 2019) or reinforcement/imitation learning (Kreutzer et al., 2018; Tan et al., 2018; Huang et al., 2019; Du and Ji, 2019) which can help alleviate exposure bias (He et al., 2019) and repetition issues, and improve handling long-term rewards; (3) selecting a decoding strategy, from classical methods like greedy decoding, beam search and random sampling up to more recent techniques like top-k (Fan et al., 2018), nucleus sampling (Holtzman et al., 2019) or penalized sampling (Keskar et al., 2019). This section will cover the material on classical techniques (30% of time) and mainly focus the recent progress on the related topics (70% of time)

3. **Break** (20 minutes)

4. **Generation with Rich Context** (25 minutes long): This section will discuss recent works on incorporating various types of context information in neural language generation. Going beyond simple context information provided by single sentence contexts, we will overview the growing body of work exploring various strategies to incorporate different types of context information either textual, e.g., syntactic, topic, and discourse information (Wang et al., 2019; Shen et al., 2019; Clark et al., 2018; Bosselut et al., 2018), or beyond text, including knowledge graph, database and images (Parthasarathi and Pineau, 2018; Dinan et al., 2018).

5. **Benchmarks and Evaluation** (30 minutes long): Given the diversity of text generation tasks and domains, it can be challenging to design reliable benchmarks and evaluation metrics (Lowe et al., 2017; Reiter, 2018; Clark et al., 2019; See et al., 2019). In this section, we will summarize the current status on these topics.

6. **Building Neural Models for Generation** (20 minutes long): This section will provide hand-on exercise, using existing deep learning packages, to build a neural language generation model. This section will also demonstrates how different learning/decoding strategies can have a strong impact on the quality of generated texts.

7. **Open problems and directions** (10 minutes long): In this final section, we will summarize the topics covered in the tutorial and point to a selection of open problems and future research directions.

4.2 Breadth

We estimate that the 30% of the tutorial will cover the recent work by the tutorial presenters, and the rest will be on cutting-research work by other researchers.

5 Information about the Presenters

Yangfeng Ji is the William Wulf Assistant Professor in the Department of Computer Science at the University of Virginia, where he leads the Natural Language Processing group. His research interests include building machine learning models for text understanding and generation. His work on entity-driven story generation won an Outstanding Paper Award at NAACL 2018.website

Antoine Bosselut is a PhD student in the Paul G. Allen School of Computer Science at the University of Washington and a Student Researcher at the Allen Institute for Artificial Intelligence (AI2). His research interests are in integrating commonsense knowledge and reasoning into downstream applications for text generation, summarization, and conversational dialogue. He regularly publishes papers at ACL, NAACL, EMNLP, and ICLR. He organized the NeuralGen workshop at NAACL 2019, and West Coast NLP (WeCNLP) in 2018 and 2019. website

Thomas Wolf leads the Science Team at Huggingface Inc., a Brooklyn-based startup working on Natural Language Generation and Understanding. He previously co-organized the NeuralGen 2019 workshop and the tutorial on Transfer Learning in NLP at NAACL 2019. His team has open-sourced several widely used libraries for coreference resolution and transfer learning in NLP and regularly publish research papers in ML and CL conferences (ICLR, ACL, AAAI...). His primary research interest is Natural Language Generation and Transfer Learning. website

Asli Celikyilmaz is Principal Researcher at Microsoft Research in Redmond, Washington. She is also an Affiliate Professor at the University of Washington. Her research interests are mainly in deep learning and natural language, specifically on long text generation, multi-document summarization, conversational modeling, human-computer interaction, and knowledge representation. She has presented several tutorials at venues including CoLing'18, ACL'17, ICASSP'17, Interspeech'17 and organized workshops at ACL, NAACL, Neurips. She has published several papers in ACL, EMNLP, NAACL, CVPR, NeurIPS, ICLR, ICASSP, IEEE TASLP, among other venues. She received several 'best of' awards including best paper award at Semantic Computing 2009, CVPR 2019. She received her Ph.D. degree from University of Toronto, Canada. website

6 Additional details

Audience Size. Based on the increasing interest in natural language generation (larger growth rate in submissions compared to other areas of NLP[1]), we anticipate that between 150 and 200 attendees will be interested in this tutorial.

Special Requirements. The tutorial will require internet access for participants to be able to access the slides and, optionally, to access hands-on coding notebooks.

Preferred Venues. Our preferred venues are EMNLP 2020, ACL 2020, and CoLing 2020.

Open Access. We agree to allow the publication of our slides and a video recording of our tutorial in the ACL Anthology. All our materials will additionally be posted on our tutorial website.

Small Reading List.

1. (Gatt and Krahmer, 2018): traditional methods on natural language generation
2. (Radford et al., 2019): large-scale language models as unsupervised multitask learners with generative capabilities
3. (Khandelwal et al., 2019): example highlighting the rise of pretrained language models for neural text generation
4. (Holtzman et al., 2019): studying the dramatic effect of decoding strategies on the quality of machine text

[1] http://acl2019pcblog.fileli.unipi.it/?p=152

5. (Kusner et al., 2015): going beyond n-gram matching, using representation learning to evaluate generation
6. (Ranzato et al., 2015): introduction to exposure bias and training with sequence-level objective functions
7. (Bowman et al., 2016): variational autoencoders for language generation
8. (Holtzman et al., 2018): designing neural networks as scoring functions during decoding

References

Samy Bengio, Oriol Vinyals, Navdeep Jaitly, and Noam Shazeer. 2015. Scheduled sampling for sequence prediction with recurrent neural networks. In *Advances in Neural Information Processing Systems*, pages 1171–1179.

Antoine Bosselut, Asli elikyilmaz, Xiaodong He, Jianfeng Gao, Po-Sen Huang, and Yejin Choi. 2018. Discourse-aware neural rewards for coherent text generation. In *Proceedings of the 16th Annual Meeting of the North American Association for Computational Linguistics (NAACL)*.

Samuel R Bowman, Luke Vilnis, Oriol Vinyals, Andrew Dai, Rafal Jozefowicz, and Samy Bengio. 2016. Generating sentences from a continuous space. In *Proceedings of The 20th SIGNLL Conference on Computational Natural Language Learning*, pages 10–21.

Elizabeth Clark, Asli Celikyilmaz, and Noah A Smith. 2019. Sentence movers similarity: Automatic evaluation for multi-sentence texts. In *Proceedings of the 57th Annual Meeting of the Association for Computational Linguistics*, pages 2748–2760.

Elizabeth Clark, Yangfeng Ji, and Noah A Smith. 2018. Neural text generation in stories using entity representations as context. In *Proceedings of the 2018 Conference of the North American Chapter of the Association for Computational Linguistics: Human Language Technologies, Volume 1 (Long Papers)*, pages 2250–2260.

Jacob Devlin, Ming-Wei Chang, Kenton Lee, and Kristina Toutanova. 2018. Bert: Pre-training of deep bidirectional transformers for language understanding. *arXiv preprint arXiv:1810.04805*.

Emily Dinan, Stephen Roller, Kurt Shuster, Angela Fan, Michael Auli, and Jason Weston. 2018. Wizard of wikipedia: Knowledge-powered conversational agents. *arXiv preprint arXiv:1811.01241*.

Wanyu Du and Yangfeng Ji. 2019. An empirical comparison on imitation learning and reinforcement learning for paraphrase generation. *arXiv preprint arXiv:1908.10835*.

Angela Fan, Mike Lewis, and Yann Dauphin. 2018. Hierarchical neural story generation. *arXiv preprint arXiv:1805.04833*.

William Fedus, Ian Goodfellow, and Andrew M Dai. 2018. Maskgan: better text generation via filling in the_. *arXiv preprint arXiv:1801.07736*.

Albert Gatt and Emiel Krahmer. 2018. Survey of the state of the art in natural language generation: Core tasks, applications and evaluation. *Journal of Artificial Intelligence Research*, 61:65–170.

Sergey Golovanov, Rauf Kurbanov, Sergey I. Nikolenko, Kyryl Truskovskyi, Alexander Tselousov, and Thomas Wolf. 2019. Large-scale transfer learning for natural language generation. In *ACL*.

Tianxing He, Jingzhao Zhang, Zhiming Zhou, and James Glass. 2019. Quantifying exposure bias for neural language generation. *arXiv preprint arXiv:1905.10617*.

Ari Holtzman, Jan Buys, Maxwell Forbes, Antoine Bosselut, David Golub, and Yejin Choi. 2018. Learning to write with cooperative discriminators. In *ACL*.

Ari Holtzman, Jan Buys, Maxwell Forbes, and Yejin Choi. 2019. The curious case of neural text degeneration. *arXiv preprint arXiv:1904.09751*.

Zhiting Hu, Zichao Yang, Xiaodan Liang, Ruslan Salakhutdinov, and Eric P Xing. 2017. Toward controlled generation of text. In *Proceedings of the 34th International Conference on Machine Learning-Volume 70*, pages 1587–1596. JMLR. org.

Qiuyuan Huang, Zhe Gan, Asli Celikyilmaz, Dapeng Wu, Jianfeng Wang, and Xiaodong He. 2019. Hierarchically structured reinforcement learning for topically coherent visual story generation. In *Proceedings of the AAAI Conference on Artificial Intelligence*, volume 33, pages 8465–8472.

Nitish Shirish Keskar, Bryan McCann, Lav R. Varshney, Caiming Xiong, and Richard Socher. 2019. Ctrl: A conditional transformer language model for controllable generation.

Urvashi Khandelwal, Kevin Clark, Dan Jurafsky, and Lukasz Kaiser. 2019. Sample efficient text summarization using a single pre-trained transformer. *arXiv preprint arXiv:1905.08836*.

Julia Kreutzer, Joshua Uyheng, and Stefan Riezler. 2018. Reliability and learnability of human bandit feedback for sequence-to-sequence reinforcement learning. *arXiv preprint arXiv:1805.10627*.

Matt J. Kusner, Yongqiang Sun, Nicholas I. Kolkin, and Kilian Q. Weinberger. 2015. From word embeddings to document distances. In *ICML*.

Jiwei Li, Will Monroe, Tianlin Shi, Alan Ritter, and Dan Jurafsky. 2017. Adversarial learning for neural dialogue generation. In *EMNLP*.

Ryan Lowe, Michael Noseworthy, Iulian Vlad Serban, Nicolas Angelard-Gontier, Yoshua Bengio, and Joelle Pineau. 2017. Towards an automatic turing test: Learning to evaluate dialogue responses. In *Proceedings of the 55th Annual Meeting of the Association for Computational Linguistics (Volume 1: Long Papers)*, pages 1116–1126.

Prasanna Parthasarathi and Joelle Pineau. 2018. Extending neural generative conversational model using external knowledge sources. In *Proceedings of the 2018 Conference on Empirical Methods in Natural Language Processing*, pages 690–695.

Alec Radford, Jeffrey Wu, Rewon Child, David Luan, Dario Amodei, and Ilya Sutskever. 2019. Language models are unsupervised multitask learners.

Marc'Aurelio Ranzato, Sumit Chopra, Michael Auli, and Wojciech Zaremba. 2015. Sequence level training with recurrent neural networks. *CoRR*, abs/1511.06732.

Ehud Reiter. 2018. A structured review of the validity of bleu. *Computational Linguistics*, 44(3):393–401.

Abigail See, Peter J. Liu, and Christopher D. Manning. 2017. Get to the point: Summarization with pointer-generator networks. In *Proceedings of the 55th Annual Meeting of the Association for Computational Linguistics*.

Abigail See, Stephen Roller, Douwe Kiela, and Jason Weston. 2019. What makes a good conversation? how controllable attributes affect human judgments. *arXiv preprint arXiv:1902.08654*.

Dinghan Shen, Asli Celikyilmaz, Yizhe Zhang, Liqun Chen, Xin Wang, Jianfeng Gao, and Lawrence Carin. 2019. Towards generating long and coherent text with multi-level latent variable models. *arXiv preprint arXiv:1902.00154*.

Sandeep Subramanian, Sai Rajeswar Mudumba, Alessandro Sordoni, Adam Trischler, Aaron C Courville, and Chris Pal. 2018. Towards text generation with adversarially learned neural outlines. In *Advances in Neural Information Processing Systems*, pages 7551–7563.

Bowen Tan, Zhiting Hu, Zichao Yang, Ruslan Salakhutdinov, and Eric Xing. 2018. Connecting the dots between mle and rl for sequence generation. *arXiv preprint arXiv:1811.09740*.

Ashish Vaswani, Noam Shazeer, Niki Parmar, Jakob Uszkoreit, Llion Jones, Aidan N Gomez, Łukasz Kaiser, and Illia Polosukhin. 2017. Attention is all you need. In *Advances in neural information processing systems*, pages 5998–6008.

Wenlin Wang, Zhe Gan, Hongteng Xu, Ruiyi Zhang, Guoyin Wang, Dinghan Shen, Changyou Chen, and Lawrence Carin. 2019. Topic-guided variational auto-encoder for text generation. In *Proceedings of the 2019 Conference of the North American Chapter of the Association for Computational Linguistics: Human Language Technologies, Volume 1 (Long and Short Papers)*, pages 166–177.

Sean Welleck, Ilia Kulikov, Stephen Roller, Emily Dinan, Kyunghyun Cho, and Jason Weston. 2019. Neural text generation with unlikelihood training. *arXiv preprint arXiv:1908.04319*.

Sam Wiseman, Stuart M. Shieber, and Alexander M. Rush. 2017. Challenges in data-to-document generation. In *EMNLP*.

Sam Wiseman, Stuart M Shieber, and Alexander M Rush. 2018. Learning neural templates for text generation. *arXiv preprint arXiv:1808.10122*.

Ziang Xie. 2017. Neural text generation: A practical guide. *arXiv preprint arXiv:1711.09534*.

Jingjing Xu, Xuancheng Ren, Yi Zhang, Qi Zeng, Xiaoyan Cai, and Xu Sun. 2018. A skeleton-based model for promoting coherence among sentences in narrative story generation. *arXiv preprint arXiv:1808.06945*.

Zachary M Ziegler, Luke Melas-Kyriazi, Sebastian Gehrmann, and Alexander M Rush. 2019. Encoder-agnostic adaptation for conditional language generation. *arXiv preprint arXiv:1908.06938*.

Association for Computational Linguistics
209 N. Eighth Street
Stroudsburg, Pennsylvania 18360

ISBN 978-1-7138-1981-3

CURRAN ASSOCIATES INC.
proceedings.com

9 781713 819813